CW01507550

# INTROD(

Did you know that the great American inventor Benjamin Franklin once accidentally blew himself up while trying to electrocute a turkey?

And did you know that the last person to leave the *Titanic* was the ship's baker?

Or how about this: Henry VIII—one of the most famous kings in history—once challenged the king of France to a wrestling match?

These are just a few of the dozens of fascinating stories you'll find here in *Captivating History for Curious Kids*.

Over the next ten chapters, we're going to take a journey back through time, covering everything from the ancient world of the Greeks and Romans to the invention of the shopper's barcode in the mid-20th century.

Along the way, we'll not only find out more about the likes of Benjamin Franklin and Henry VIII but we'll also meet husband and wife pirates, a woman who claimed to have given birth to a litter of rabbits, the explorer who gave the world the humble potato—and a whole lot more!

So, let's get started, shall we? We'll begin by traveling more than 2,000 years into the past, with some opening tales all about life in the ancient world.

# CAPTIVATING HISTORY FOR CURIOUS KIDS

## AN AWESOME HISTORY BOOK FOR KIDS WITH UNBELIEVABLE STORIES AND FACTS ABOUT THE STRANGE WORLD WE LIVE IN

**JORDAN MOORE**

ISBN: 979-8-88768-031-6

Copyright © 2025 by Red Panda Press

ALL RIGHTS RESERVED

No part of this book may be reproduced, stored in a retrieval system, or transmitted in any form or by any means, electronic, mechanical, photocopying, recording, scanning, or otherwise, without the prior written permission of the publisher.

# CONTENTS

# CHAPTER 1:
# FIRST & FOREMOST

# THE FIRST TELEPHONE CALL

Long before we were all connected to one another online and by telephone, sending a letter through the mail was, by far, the best and fastest way to get a message to someone.

But as our transportation and technologies improved—with larger and faster ships ferrying letters across the ocean more quickly and steam trains replacing horses and ponies over land—the speed of sending written letters through the mail improved too. Even still, it could often take many days, if not many weeks, for the mail to reach its destination. Plus, there was always the risk of paper envelopes and messages going missing or being lost in accidents along the way!

In the mid-1800s, however, all that began to change. It was then that we began to be able to communicate electronically, using wires and radio waves, and therefore send messages to one another in a matter of moments.

The first system along these lines was the telegraph—an early 19th-century invention in which simple electronic tones and beeps could be used to relay coded messages over vast distances. Then, in 1876, a Scottish inventor named Alexander Graham Bell, working in a laboratory in Boston, Massachusetts, was granted the patent for the world's very first telephone.

The idea behind Bell's invention was fairly simple, but the technology was very complicated! In simple terms, as the sound of a person's voice moves through the air, the air responds by moving and fluctuating with it to produce a sound wave. Bell believed that a current of electricity could be used in exactly the same way. The sound of a person's voice would be fed into an electronic system through a microphone-like receiver, and the sound wave it produced would then be used to change the shape of the electric current, just like it would if it were moving through the air!

All that was needed at the other end of the system was a receiver with which to switch these changes in current back into sound. Bell thought that using a system along these lines, a person would be able to send not just beeps and tones down an electric cable but their own voice instead.

Just three days after his patent was granted, on March 10, 1876, Bell made a breakthrough in his Boston laboratory. Having constructed a prototype telephone (which he simply called an "instrument"), Bell lifted the receiver to his mouth and spoke into it. His assistant, Thomas Watson, was in another room nearby, holding the instrument's receiver. And through it, he heard the world's first telephone call: "Mr. Watson, come here—I want to see you."

Bell's voice was crackly, a little quiet, and rather unclear, but the system had nevertheless worked. Over the months (and eventually years) that followed, he continued to improve his telephone and the quality of its sound. The following year, the Bell Telephone Company was founded to bring this new technology to the market.

# THE FIRST WORD SENT OVER THE INTERNET

Another form of communication that is easy to take for granted is the internet.

These days, we can send emails and messages online in a matter of moments, with people anywhere in the world able to read them and reply—even sending voice notes, photographs, and videos—so long as they, too, are connected to the World Wide Web.

Back in the 1960s, however, things were very different. Only a tiny handful of researchers scattered across the United States were looking into online communication. All they had at their disposal to connect to other researchers looking into the same field was an early ancestor of the modern internet system called the US Advanced Research Projects Agency Network, or ARPANET.

The ARPANET was overseen by a branch of the US Defense Department and was partly funded by the Pentagon. Its aim was to send written messages without using existing telephone connections, which could easily be tapped and secretly listened to by spies and other undercover agents. This was especially important at the height of America's so-called "Cold War" conflict with Russia.

Using a new computerized network would allow so-called "packets" of digital information—which could be "unpacked" as text at the receiving end of the message—to be sent safely. With ARPANET bases in universities and education centers across America, however, the network's potential as a way for scientists and other researchers, located hundreds of miles from one another, to instantly send each other papers, documents, and other written works using the network soon became clear. As such, the purpose of the network soon shifted from helping the military to helping teachers and university staff.

As the technology slowly improved, it finally became time to test this new online world. Late in the evening on Wednesday, October 29, 1969, a grad student named Charley Kline, studying at the University of California, Los Angeles, sat down at a UCLA computer and began typing the word "LOGIN" into the university's ARPANET system.

Unfortunately, the system was quickly overloaded with data, and it crashed after he had managed to write just two letters! As a result, the very first message ever sent over the internet was a meaningless "L-O." About an hour later, however, Kline was able to reset the system and input the full word—LOGIN— at around 11:30 p.m. The message was sent successfully, and his computer managed to connect with another computer around 350 miles further up the Californian coast, at the Stanford Research Institute.

These days, of course, things have moved on quite a bit; as of 2025, around 400 terabytes of new data are created online every single day. Around half of that traffic is generated by online videos and video messages alone!

Back in 1969, however, the system Kline was working with had just 128 kilobytes of memory and only 24 megabytes of disk space. That meant the entire internet at that time was more than 16 million times smaller than the amount of data we now send around the world every 24 hours!

## THE FIRST SELFIE

These days, anyone who has a smartphone can take a selfie whenever they want to and send it to their friends or post it online in an instant. Back in the early days of photography, however, things weren't quite so instantaneous...

Almost 200 years ago, in the early 1800s, cameras had no digital displays, no autofocusing lenses, nor any batteries, flashes, or electrical components to work them. Instead, many early photographic devices were far more practical and relied on the photographer mixing up a special combination of light-sensitive chemicals coated onto thin sheets of metal, glass, or paper.

When this sheet of chemicals was then exposed to a controlled amount of light—with a lens used to focus the image onto the glass—the chemicals in this special coating changed color to produce a permanent picture on the surface. In the very early days of photography, however, these chemicals were not particularly strong or reliable. It could often take several minutes for them to respond enough for a permanent picture to be taken.

During that time, anything that moved or did not keep still in front of the lens would either appear blurred in the final picture or, if moving particularly quickly, would simply not show up at all. Understandably, this made taking pictures of people very tricky, as the person being photographed was required to stay absolutely still for many minutes at a time. Otherwise, they would ruin the photograph, and the process would have to be started again!

In 1839, however, an early pioneer of the photographic process named Robert Cornelius not only managed to take the first known clear portrait but also somehow managed to turn his camera around on himself. That's right—he took the world's first selfie!

Cornelius was working in his family's gaslighting business in Philadelphia when he first became interested in photography. He made his own makeshift camera, using an old pair of opera glasses—a kind of ornate pair of binoculars used by theatregoers for seeing the action on stage up close from far away in the audience—to make the lens.

He then mixed up the required light-sensitive chemicals and coated a sheet of metal with them before setting up his camera in the family yard, relying on nothing more than sunlight to develop the picture. Next, he sat in front of the camera for a full 15 minutes, remaining completely motionless the entire time to give the metal plate sufficient time and sunlight to work its magic. Once the 15 minutes were up, he then covered the camera lens, stopping more light from entering and ruining the picture, and removed the plate.

The result was not just a perfectly clear image of Cornelius—with tousled dark hair and a high white shirt collar—but the very first portrait, and the very first selfie, in photographic history!

## THE FIRST ANIMAL IN SPACE

It's not a very nice fact, but it's often the case that scientists and researchers need to test their new inventions and technologies on animals before deciding if they're safe enough for people to use them as well.

From makeup to medicine, laboratory animals like these have been doing their bit to help our understanding of science for centuries—including during the famous "Space Race" of the mid-1900s.

When it comes to testing potentially risky technologies, few ideas are more dangerous than using a super-powered spacecraft to blast off from the surface of the Earth with enough speed to escape the Earth's gravitational pull and rise high enough in the air to enter space! As a result, long before astronauts began donning space suits and stepping onto rocket ships, the very first living things ever sent into space on board early test flights were animals.

In the 1940s and '50s, when the United States and Soviet Union began their competition to explore outer space, both nations launched several early missions and test flights with animals on board. In the very early days of the Space Race, rockets containing rabbits, mice, fruit flies, and even monkeys were sent miles up into the atmosphere and beyond. This was a means of testing both the safety of the spacecraft being developed and the potential dangers of traveling outside the Earth's atmosphere. (Radiation from the sun is far stronger in space than it is here on Earth, and scientists were not sure how safe space travel would even be as a result!)

Although fruit flies had been used on the very earliest flights to reach the limits of space, those early flights were mainly long-distance missile tests organized by the military. As such, they were not part of official space missions. Instead, the first animal intentionally sent into outer space was a rhesus monkey named Albert, who was launched some 83 miles above the Earth on board an American rocket, called V2, from Holloman Air Force Base, in New Mexico, in June 1949.

Albert's space flight, however, simply went straight up and straight back down again. Once V2 reached its highest height, it simply fell back toward Earth and parachuted to the ground. The first animal to complete a full orbit of the Earth—performing the first true space flight in the process—was, in fact, a dog.

Having already tested one spacecraft in an orbit around the Earth, Soviet cosmonauts in Russia launched their Sputnik 2 spacecraft in 1957. On board was a stray mongrel picked up from the streets of Moscow, which the team of researchers named Laika (a Russian word meaning "barker").

On November 3, Laika and *Sputnik 2* were launched into low orbit from a space station in the Russian city of Baikonur (now in Kazakhstan). The spacecraft began circling the Earth in outer space. Reaching a maximum distance from the Earth of over 1,000 miles, *Sputnik 2* circled the planet successfully in just 103 minutes, before continuing to orbit again and again.

The flight was an astonishing success, with the Russian cosmonauts back on Earth using a complex system of monitors to measure everything from the temperature and radiation levels on board, to Laika's heartrate and breathing. Laika had food and water on board, but sadly, as the technology was still in its very earliest days at the time, conditions proved too much and Laika died during *Sputnik 2's* fourth orbit of the Earth.

We learned an awful lot from Laika's time in space, however, and her hugely important role in making space travel safe and possible has led to her name going down in history.

## THE FIRST WOMAN TO FLY THE ATLANTIC

It's easy to think of the greatest achievements and amazing feats of world exploration as being something of a man's world.

From Marco Polo to Christopher Columbus, almost all the great explorers of history were male. And many of the great feats of modern exploration—from climbing Mount Everest to reaching the South Pole—were likewise achieved by men.

In the early days of aviation, however, that wasn't quite the case. Although Charles Lindbergh was by far the most famous aircraft pilot of the time, he had stiff competition from an expert female aviator named Amelia Earhart.

Born in Kansas in 1897, Earhart worked as a nurse during World War I before relocating to California with her family in 1920. It was then that she went on her first airplane ride, and she soon became obsessed with the idea of becoming a pilot herself. The following year, she bought her first airplane, and over the years that followed, Earhart racked up countless hours of flying experience.

By this time, flying was becoming a worldwide industry. Aviators and pioneers all around the globe were achieving ever longer, ever more daring, and ever more impressive flying firsts. And chief among them was the American pilot, Charles Lindbergh.

Lindbergh began his flying career in the army before working as a flight teacher, stunt pilot, and airmail deliverer in the years after the war. Then, in 1927, he and his single-engine monoplane, the *Spirit of St. Louis*, entered the so-called Orteig Prize—a long-running (and potentially hugely dangerous) contest with a $25,000 prize for the first pilot to fly successfully from New York to Paris.

Just after 7:00 a.m. on May 20, Lindbergh took off from Roosevelt Field on Long Island, New York. He touched down on the outskirts of Paris, some 3,600 miles away, just over 33 hours later.

Lindbergh's transatlantic flight made headlines all around the world, and before long, others were looking to emulate it—including Amelia Earhart. A little over a year later, she took off from Newfoundland, Canada, on board a seaplane co-piloted by flying duo Wilmer Stultz and Louis Gordon. Together, the team of three touched down in Wales, UK, around 20 hours later.

That 1928 flight might have made Earhart the first woman to fly across the Atlantic—and an international celebrity in the process!—but she wasn't ready to hang up her flying goggles quite yet. Instead, she became determined to complete the same flight on her own, and in May 1932, Earhart flew from Newfoundland to Northern Ireland in a record time of 14 hours and 56 minutes—more than halving Lindbergh's time and becoming the first woman to fly solo across the Atlantic Ocean!

In the years that followed, Earhart continued to perform extraordinary feats of aviation, setting new records in height and speed and even becoming the first woman to fly solo across the Pacific, too.

In 1937, however, she and her aircraft disappeared while attempting to complete a record-breaking journey flying around the world. It is presumed that her plane crashed somewhere in the Pacific Ocean. Although there have long been rumors that Earhart perhaps brought her plane down on an isolated island and remained there the rest of her life, the true fate of one of the world's greatest ever aviators and explorers remains unknown.

## DID YOU KNOW?

○ The first people to summit Mount Everest were the New Zealand mountaineer Edmund Hillary and his Sherpa guide Tenzing Norgay. They reached the peak at 11:30 a.m. on May 29, 1953.

○ The first explorer to cross the Antarctic Circle was Captain Cook in 1773.

○ The first hot air balloon flight, in 1783, took place a full 120 years before the Wright Brothers made the first airplane flight!

○ In 1947, the pilot Chuck Yaeger became the first person in history to fly faster than the speed of sound.

○ The first patent ever permitted in the United States was for a process for making the industrial chemical potash in 1790.

○ The first modern Olympic Games were held in Athens in 1896.

○ The first food ever microwaved was a bag of popcorn.

- The first text message ever sent was in 1992. It said, "Merry Christmas!"
- The first building ever referred to as a "skyscraper" was built in Chicago in 1884. It only had ten stories!
- Yellowstone was America's first national park and was officially opened to the public in 1872.

# CHAPTER 2:
# GREECE & ROME

# THE BATTLE OF THERMOPYLAE

From the Trojan War to the Battle of Actium—which saw the Romans defeat Queen Cleopatra of Egypt!—the ancient world played host to a huge number of wars and battles.

Some of these were truly remarkable. When Hannibal, the great ruler of the ancient state of Carthage, launched an attack on Rome in the 3rd century BCE, for instance, he did so by marching an army of war elephants through the great snowy mountains of the Alps!

Of all the wars and battles of the ancient world, though, perhaps the most unlikely—in terms of the sheer number of soldiers and fighters involved—was the Battle of Thermopylae.

The battle took place in the summer of 480 BCE between an allied group of Ancient Greek states and the invading Persian army, led by Xerxes I. The cause of the battle was something that had happened more than a decade earlier, under the rule of Xerxes' father, Darius the Great.

As one of the most powerful leaders of the time, Darius had set his sights on conquering Greece. He had sent messengers and heralds from Persia (in modern-day Iran) to the major city-states of Greece, proposing that they join his ever-growing empire. The cities of Athens and Sparta, however, did not take kindly to Darius' quiet attempt to take control of them—and as a sign of their displeasure, they threw his messengers into a pit!

When word of what had happened got back to Persia, Darius was understandably furious. He vowed to take control of both Sparta and Athens, no matter what it took. After Darius' death in 486 BCE, his son Xerxes took over his father's quest and launched his attack on Greece just six years later.

Xerxes' armies moved quickly and were soon in control of much of northern Greece. The remaining cities and states of the south of Greece joined forces as best they could, and they eventually brought together a combined army of around 7,000 (mainly Spartan) soldiers. Xerxes' armies, however, numbered more than 40 times that number, with some records from the time suggesting the Persians had more than 300,000 men. Despite the huge difference in the size of the two sides, however, the Greeks were determined to defend their land—and what's more, they knew exactly where best to do it!

To the north of Athens lay a narrow strip of land called Thermopylae. Only a few yards wide, the strip of land straddled the sea on one side and an impossibly steep hillside on the other. Knowing that the Persians would have no choice but to take this narrow route into southern Greece, the Greeks concentrated all their forces on Thermopylae. There, they managed to hold back Xerxes' immense army for a full two days.

The Greek defense might well have held longer, in fact, were it not for a sly Greek soldier named Ephialtes. Wanting to curry favor with the Persians, he sneaked away from his fellow Greeks and secretly met with Xerxes, giving him and his men directions to a secret route around Thermopylae. With the Greeks now double-crossed and the Persians now attacking from both sides, many of the Greeks were forced to retreat. However, a lone band of around 300 Spartan soldiers continued fighting, holding back Xerxes' thousands of men as long as possible.

Eventually, however, the sheer size of the Persian forces proved too great. The remaining Spartans were overwhelmed, and Xerxes and his forces marched on and took control of much of mainland Greece, extending his enormous empire by hundreds of miles. The brave attempt of this tiny group of Spartan soldiers to hold his armies back, however, has made the Battle of Thermopylae one of the most extraordinary and memorable battles in ancient history.

## THE YEAR OF FOUR EMPERORS

Dozens of men ruled as Emperor of Rome during the centuries that the Roman Empire dominated much of Europe—from Emperor Augustus in 27 BCE, through to the final emperor, Romulus, in 476 CE.

Many of these emperors ruled for a great many years. The infamous emperor Nero reigned for 13 years, as did his predecessor, Claudius. The emperor Hadrian—known for building an immense wall across the north of England—ruled for a full two decades, from 117 to 138 CE. And as well as being its first emperor, Augustus was also the Roman Empire's longest-serving ruler, remaining on the throne for more than 40 years.

At the opposite end of the scale, however, some Roman emperors were in power for just a matter of months, or even weeks. And in 69 CE, Rome saw no less than four different emperors all crowned inside a single year!

The so-called "Year of the Four Emperors" began with the death of Emperor Nero the previous summer. He committed suicide after his increasingly bizarre and unpredictable behavior led to him being labeled an enemy of the Roman state. Nero's successor, the emperor Galba, was one of those who had been involved in his downfall. In the process, Galba had been made ready for power and encouraged to challenge Nero by several high-ranking Roman generals.

Galba, however, was old and had no children, and as such had no heir to replace him after he died. This made him unpopular, both with the Roman senate and the Roman people. When Galba overlooked a popular general, named Otho, in favor of another, named Lucius, as his successor and heir, Otho soon began plotting his downfall.

In January 69 CE, Otho murdered Galba and assumed the throne himself. He soon proved a far more popular leader than Galba had been. Even still, not everyone was convinced he was the right man for the job! Before long, rebellions and protests began breaking out across the empire, in particular in the northern and central regions of Europe. There, a Roman legion in central France threw their support behind a new leader, named Vitellius, and began plotting to ensure he became emperor instead.

Forces loyal to Vitellius rose up in Europe, and in April 69 CE, they clashed with Otho's troops at the town of Bedriacum, in northern Italy. The battle was an embarrassing disaster for Otho, who lost tens of thousands of men. Many of those who retreated and survived the battle abandoned their support for him and pledged themselves to Vitellius instead. Seeing no chance of returning to Rome or securing victory, Otho took his own life. That left Vitellius free to sweep to power and claim the throne for himself as Rome's third emperor in just four months!

Just when the empire was in desperate need of some calm, however, a fourth challenger entered the scene. In the far east of Europe, a general named Vespasian began rallying the Roman legions around the famous river Danube. Before long, support for him was growing across the empire.

With people who had been loyal to both Galba and Otho in the past now also throwing their support behind him, Vespasian marched on Rome. He challenged Vitellius to a battle, again in the town of Bedriacum. This time, it was Vitellius who was defeated, and as the year came to an end, Vespasian was left to take the throne—as Rome's fourth emperor in a single year!

# THE VICTORY OF PYRRHUS

Have you ever heard the expression a *pyrrhic victory?*

It's a strange turn of phrase that describes a success that comes at an enormous price to the person who succeeds.

A football team that wins a match, for instance, might be said to have won a pyrrhic victory if, in doing so, they suffered several injuries to their players or took on one too many penalties or suspensions. But did you know that this phrase refers to an actual victory in the ancient world that proved so costly that it eventually led to a king's downfall?

King Pyrrhus was ruler of Epirus, a region of Ancient Greece, who came to the throne at age 12, in 306 BCE. Because he was so young, however, he struggled to hold on to power. Just four years later, Pyrrhus was dethroned and forced to flee Greece for nearby Macedonia.

There, Pyrrhus became friends with the young prince of Macedonia, named Demetrius. Together, they traveled widely across Europe and Asia, fighting battles and making powerful friends (and enemies!) as they went. Eventually, Pyrrhus decided to return home, and in 297 BCE, he arrived back in Epirus and managed to reclaim his throne. But now, he wanted revenge.

Having traveled the world and fought in a great many battles, Pyrrhus was determined to fight off those who had ousted him from power and use his military experience to expand his empire. As a result, he and his armies began to

23

invade surrounding nations and states, fighting battle after battle across the ancient world and securing victory after victory over a string of opponents.

Each victory, however, came at immense cost. In 280 BCE, for instance, Pyrrhus launched a long campaign against nearby Rome, sailing an army of some 25,000 of his best men across the sea to Italy. There, he fought the Romans in the Battle of Heraclea. Although Pyrrhus was victorious and took a huge number of Roman soldiers captive, more than half of his own army was killed in the fighting. Some historians believe that, in this single battle alone, the king lost perhaps as many as 13,000 of his men.

Still, Pyrrhus was determined to continue his campaign against Rome. The following year, he launched a new attack at the town of Asculum. Again, he secured victory but lost many thousands more of his best fighters in the process, too. Battle after battle went like this, with Pyrrhus never quite securing enough of a victory to defeat Rome entirely, and yet always winning on the battlefield. "Another such victory as this," it is believed he once said after a battle, "and we shall be utterly ruined."

Eventually, after a naval battle off the coast of Sicily in which he lost more than 100 ships, Pyrrhus' wasteful victories proved too much. He was forced to abandon his campaigns in Italy and return home—his name forever associated with a victory that comes at too great a price.

## THE DESTRUCTION OF POMPEII

It is one of the most famous disasters in history. The eruption of Mount Vesuvius on the coast of southwest Italy in 79 CE sent immense clouds of ash and stone into the atmosphere, destroying several nearby towns and villages. Most famously of all, it ruined the Roman coastal town of Pompeii.

Long before that fateful day, the area around Mount Vesuvius had been plagued by earthquakes and tremors, with a particularly strong quake damaging nearby buildings and towns as far back as 62 CE. We know now that these increasingly powerful tremors were caused by the enormous chamber beneath the volcano slowly growing in size, as ever more molten rock was pushed up to the surface. Eventually, just after midday on August 24, 79 CE, the pressure beneath the volcano proved too much. An immense explosion showered a huge amount of rock, pebbles, and ash across Pompeii and the surrounding towns.

Incredibly, the eruption rumbled on like this for the next 12 hours, during which time the volcano continued to rain down scorching rocks and stones onto the town. Even more devastatingly, it billowed out clouds of poisonous, scalding hot gas. Many of the people in the town were either trapped or crushed inside buildings that became weighed down with rock and ash or else became overwhelmed with the poisonous fumes that followed. What little remained of them and their homes and businesses was eventually covered in a thick blanket of ash as much as 19 ft deep.

Because the entire town was lost to the volcano, Pompeii and its surrounding towns of Stabiae and Herculaneum were eventually forgotten about. It would not be for more than 1,600 years, in the 18th century, that the ruins of the town were at long last rediscovered.

## LIVIA DRUSILLA, THE MURDERESS OF ANCIENT ROME

Roman history is, of course, full of famous (and infamous!) people, from Julius Caesar and his general Mark Anthony to the likes of Emperors Nero, Claudius, and Caligula. One of the Roman Empire's less widely known characters, however, was Livia Drusilla, or Julia Augusta—the wife of the very first Roman emperor, Caesar Augustus.

Livia was born in 59 BCE, the daughter of a high-ranking Roman senator named Marcus Claudianus. Through his connections in the senate, when she was just 16 years old, Livia married a senator named Tiberius Claudius Nero. They had a son, also named Tiberius. Just five years later, however, Tiberius and Livia's marriage broke apart, the couple divorced, and Livia married an increasingly powerful political leader named Octavian.

Then, in 27 BCE, Octavian was elected the very first emperor of Rome, adopting the new name Augustus in the process. His young stepson Tiberius, therefore, became his heir, and Livia became Rome's first-ever empress.

As the wife of the emperor, Livia got to know a lot about how Rome worked, and she would discuss the comings and goings of the city with her husband. Eventually, she too became very powerful and had a lot of influence over the empire. According to some historians, though, Livia did far more than that. There were rumors in Rome that she would stop at nothing to ensure that she and her husband remained in power and that her son Tiberius remained the empire's only heir.

Throughout the 40 years Augustus ruled over Rome, Livia is said to have banished or even murdered a great many of her husband's rivals and potential successors to make sure that Tiberius remained first in line to the throne. One story even claims that when Augustus began to think his grandson, not his stepson, should succeed him instead, Livia had Augustus killed, too!

How much of that story is true—and indeed, how much of any of the bloodthirsty stories about Livia's life are true!—is not known. Although some historians believe them, others think that stories like these are just gossip, written down at the time by people in Ancient Rome who did not like Livia and were determined to ruin her reputation.

In her defense, for instance, Livia was known for her charitableness and mercy, and on more than one occasion is even known to have asked Augustus to free prisoners who had been sentenced to death. Whether any of this is true or not, however, Livia is by far one of Rome's most interesting characters!

## DID YOU KNOW?

O Rome was the first city in history to be home to one million people.

O One of the chemicals the Romans used to keep their toga robes bright white was obtained from human pee!

O To avoid getting drunk, the Ancient Greeks would water down their wine. During the winter, it was customary to use fresh snow instead!

O References to specific colors are so rare in Ancient Greek literature that some historians in the 19th century believed the Greeks might have all been color blind!

O Roman gladiators weren't all sword fighters. In fact, there were lots of different kinds of gladiators, each named for their weaponry or fighting technique— including a retiarus (who carried a net), a parmularius (who carried a small shield), and a sagittarius (who used a bow and arrow).

O According to legend, Rome was founded by—and named after—two orphaned brothers named Romulus and Remus, who were raised by a wolf.

- The Romans sometimes deliberately flooded the Colosseum so that they could stage fake sea battles in front of the crowd.
- Ancient Greek women were surprisingly modern. They used makeup, perfume, hair pomade—and even used flint stones to shave their legs!
- Only the very wealthiest Romans wore togas. The usual day-to-day clothing of most people was a simple sleeveless garment called a tunic.
- The Ancient Greeks believed a man going bald was a sign of his intelligence.

# CHAPTER 3:
# INVENTORS & INVENTIONS

# LOUIS BRAILLE AND WRITING FOR THE BLIND

Braille, the brainchild and namesake of the 19th-century French inventor Louis Braille, is a unique system of reading for the blind. It uses a system of six raised pimple-like dots arranged in two columns of three dots each. These are pressed into a sheet of paper and can be read using the fingers.

In the Braille writing system, each letter of the alphabet (as well as numbers, mathematical signs, punctuation marks, and all manner of other signs and symbols) is represented using a unique combination of these six dots. Ultimately, almost any written text—and even musical notation and mathematical formulas!—can be read by people who cannot see by simply running their finger across the page and "reading" the dots one letter at a time.

But how did Louis Braille come up with such an ingenious idea in the first place?

Amazingly, a freak accident in childhood left Louis Braille blind himself—a disability that he simply refused to let hold him back.

He was just three years old when he suffered an injury to his eye in the workshop of his father, who was a maker of riding equipment. While playing with offcuts of leather, Louis tried to pierce a hole in one of them but lost control of the blade and ended up stabbing himself in his eye. Despite treatment from a local doctor, the wound became infected, and as the condition worsened, Louis gradually lost his sight.

Despite his blindness, Louis was encouraged to live as normal a life as possible. With his family's help, he grew up to be a wildly intelligent, creative, and inquisitive young man.

As a teenager, he was accepted into an important school in Paris that had been opened just for blind students like him. It was there that he began devising the writing system that would eventually make him known around the world.

The books at the Paris school were all written in a system that used wires to scratch or indent letters of the alphabet into the pages. Although this system worked, the letters had to be large enough to tell apart easily—which made the books in turn larger and heavier, and slower to read! Hearing of newer writing systems for the blind that used dots instead of letters, Louis decided to combine the two approaches and came up with his simple system of six dots. These could be used to write any letter, number, or symbol required in a short, but no less readable, way.

Ingeniously, Louis used simpler patterns of dots for more common letters, like E and A, while setting aside more complex patterns for less frequently encountered letters, like Q and J. Common combinations of letters, like TH, were likewise given their own unique combination of dots, making the reading process even faster.

After several years' work and development, Louis introduced his system in 1829. It quickly caught on and has been used by blind people—with only a handful of changes and updates over the decades—ever since.

## ALEXANDER CUMMING AND THE MODERN TOILET

Lots of inventions have had a big impact on the modern world. Some, such as the internet, computers, and mobile telephones, are recent; others, such as wheels, tools, and even metals like iron and bronze, are far, far older. But of all the inventions without which the modern world would be unlivable, perhaps the easiest to forget about is the simple flushing toilet. So, who do we have to thank for that?

The Romans famously built sewage systems beneath their cities so that waste from people's homes could be safely and cleanly moved away from built-up areas. By medieval times, separate toilets or "privies" were being added to castles and large homes so that people could conduct their business in private into a communal pit below. Finally, the very first toilet flush—that is, a swill of clean water used to clean the bowl after use—was invented in the time of the English queen Elizabeth I, more than 400 years ago.

From there, though, it was another few centuries before toilets, as we know them today, began to emerge. We can thank an Edinburgh-born Scottish inventor named Alexander

Cumming for one of the biggest steps forward in keeping us clean and healthy when we're in the bathroom!

Although he was a watchmaker and clock repairer by trade, in 1775, Cumming patented a design for the world's first flushing toilet. Although his design changed the shape of the toilet seat and bowl slightly, Cumming's most important addition to the toilet was a simple S-shaped pipe, or U-bend, hidden beneath the toilet seat among its plumbing and workings. This pipe was shaped in just such a way that when the toilet was flushed with clean water, some of that water would settle in the pipe, beneath the toilet bowl.

It was an ingenious development, as the water here would naturally form a perfect seal in the toilet pipe and therefore stop any foul smells or gases from the sewers below from drifting back up the pipe into people's homes. In fact, Cumming's invention was so significant that this simple, water-filled, S-shaped pipe is still a common fixture of all flush toilets around the world!

## THE RUBIK'S CUBE

Have you ever tried to solve a Rubik's cube?

These puzzles consist of a set of interlocking blocks, arranged in six three-by-three squares of different colors on each of the cube's faces. Twisting and rotating different three-by-three combinations of these blocks causes the colors to become jumbled, with the player then challenged to twist and turn the squares back into their original pattern.

As simple as that idea might seem—and given that some people can solve jumbled cubes in a matter of seconds!—the layout of a Rubik's cube means that there is a staggering 43 million million million different ways of scrambling it.

The Rubik's cube itself is named after its Hungarian inventor, Erno Rubik. A trained sculptor and artist, Rubik was working as a professor of design at the Budapest Academy of Arts when, in 1974, he built an early prototype of his puzzle cube using 27 interconnected wooden blocks, or "cubies." Having jumbled it up, it took Rubik himself more than a month to solve it!

Seeing the potential in his toy (which he originally called the "Magic Cube"), Rubik continued to refine its design. In 1975, he patented the mechanism inside the cube that controls the cubies' movement, and before long, he had brought the puzzle to market in Hungary.

In 1979, the cube had proved successful enough in Hungary to gain international attention. Rubik took his puzzle to various toy fairs around the world, including in London, Paris, and New York. Newly named the Rubik's cube in its inventor's honor, by 1980 more than 100 million of the puzzles had been sold worldwide!

# HOW THE WORLD CAME TO USE BARCODES

On June 26, 1974, a shopkeeper in Troy, Ohio, scanned the barcode on the back of a packet of Wrigley's chewing gum and handed it back to the customer. It's the kind of thing that happens in stores and shops all over the world day after day, but there was something quite unusual about that one almost five decades ago. This was the first time anyone had scanned a retail barcode—known at the time as a UPC, or "universal product code"—in history!

These days, of course, barcodes and similar black-and-white scanning codes are a part of modern life. Billions upon billions of them are scanned around the world every day. But did you know that this simple bit of tech dates all the way back to the 1940s?

The barcode was the brainchild of an American inventor named Joe Woodland. In 1947, he had an idea that a unique visual code that could be scanned or "read" by a machine could be used to identify individual products in a shop and thereby speed up the checkout process.

Working with a friend and fellow engineer named Bob Silver, Woodland figured out that a system of differently sized black and white lines would be the easiest way to create a unique pattern. The design he originally patented was for a circular code, consisting of a pattern of different sized circles nestled inside one another. The idea was that a circular code could be read from any angle, regardless of how the product was held.

Woodland patented his design in 1952, but with no notion of how these codes could be read, he was not able to progress it for another eight years. In 1960, however, the world's first laser beam—a concentrated beam of light—was invented. Woodland and Silver at last saw the potential in using a beam of light as a means of "reading" their codes.

As luck would have it, at that time, a research team working at RCA (the Radio Corporation of America) was looking for projects that might be able to use their laser technology, and they stumbled across Woodland and Silver's idea. The group began to collaborate on producing a new code reader and developed an early prototype that was tested in a handful of stores in 1972.

If these codes were ever going to take off, however, the RCA team knew that they needed as many retailers as possible to use them. Over the next two years, they worked with dozens of other tech companies (including a team from IBM!) to improve the code reader's design and convince retailers across America to use it.

Eventually, it was decided that a simpler, smaller, rectangular pattern of lines would be the easiest to replicate across multiple products (as, unlike a circle, it could be cut down in size while still remaining scannable!). After several further tests and countless improvements in the laser-scanning technology, the new bar-shaped code was finally rolled out in 1974 and scanned for the very first time on that morning in June.

## HOW A PLANT INSPIRED THE INVENTION OF VELCRO

Velcro is a two-sided fabric, often used in long strips or patches, that consists of a soft, wool-like texture on one side and a sharper, coarse texture made up of hundreds of tiny hook-shaped projections on the other. Pressing the two halves together causes these fabric hooks to connect with loops and tangles in the softer, woollier fabric, holding the two together. Appropriately enough, the name *Velcro* comes from a French word that literally means "hooked velvet"!

It's a simple technology that you'll find everywhere from baby harnesses to mountaineering gear. But did you know that Velcro was inspired by a plant?

It was back in 1941 that an engineer in Switzerland named George de Mestral went for a walk in the Swiss Alps with his pet dog, Milka. When he returned home, de Mestral happened to notice that lots of seed burs from the local alpine burdock plant had stuck to his woolen socks and coat—as well as to Milka's fur! Taking a closer look at the burs, de Mestral saw that they were covered in lots of tiny prong-like hooks, and it was the curled ends of these hooks that caused the seeds to stick to the furry fabric.

De Mestral was intrigued by his findings and began to think of ways in which such a design could be made and used in the modern world. A fabric consisting of hooks and loops on opposite sides, he decided, could be used as a simple fastening. He took early sketches and descriptions of his design to the weaving center of Europe, Lyon in southern France, to see if anyone there would be interested in making his design a reality.

Unfortunately, early prototypes of de Mestral's design—made using simple strips of cotton—quickly became frayed. Despite his weavers' best efforts, no working version of his idea could be made. The invention of manmade fibers, however, changed all of that.

De Mestral soon discovered that, when sewn under a special infrared light, nylon fabric naturally formed lots of tiny loop-shaped projections. To create the matching hooks, de Mestral simply cut the tops off some of the loops, creating two opposite sides, hooks and loops, that could be stuck together.

Mechanizing this process so that his new connecting fabric could be made in large quantities took another eight years of work. Eventually, his Velcro fabric was brought to market, and it has become one of the modern world's most important fabric inventions in the decades since.

## DID YOU KNOW?

- The Slinky toy was invented by accident when a metal spring fell off a shelf.
- The man who founded the Nobel Prizes, Swedish chemist and engineer Alfred Nobel, was the inventor of dynamite.
- Thomas Edison proposed to his wife using Morse code...
- ...and nicknamed his two eldest children, Marion and Thomas, Jr., "Dot" and "Dash."
- Venetian blinds weren't invented in Venice. They actually come from Japan!
- And French fries were likely invented not in France, but in neighboring Belgium!
- The words "volt" and "voltage" take their name from an Italian inventor named Count Alessandro Volta, who invented the first battery in the 18th century.
- The charcoal blocks that are used in barbecues were invented by motorcar pioneer Henry Ford.
- Rudolph Diesel, the inventor of the diesel engine, disappeared under mysterious circumstances from a ferry crossing the English Channel in 1913.
- John Deere, the founder of a famous company making farming machinery, was a blacksmith by trade.

# CHAPTER 4:
# PIRATES & SWASHBUCKLERS

# THE GENTLEMAN PIRATE

Many famous pirates and adventurers from the age of sail lived extraordinary lives even before they began their lifetime of swashbuckling and piracy. But one of the most peculiar life stories is that of the so-called "Gentleman Pirate," Stede Bonnet.

Bonnet was born in Barbados in the late 1680s. At the time, Barbados was under the control of the English, and like many of his fellow islanders, Stede came from a family of wealthy local colonial landowners. After his father's death in 1694, Bonnet inherited the family estate. For the next 20 years, he lived a life of luxury on his paradise island.

For reasons that have puzzled historians for decades, however, in 1717, Bonnet abandoned his life of leisure, purchased a sailboat he named the *Revenge*, hired a crew (whom he paid out of his own family's fortune), and embarked on a life of piracy around the Caribbean and the eastern United States.

Bonnet and his crew first sailed northwards to Jamaica, then on to the coast of mainland America, pillaging ships as far north as Virginia and New York. In August 1717, however, he made the mistake of attacking an enormous Spanish vessel off the coast of Florida, which resulted in a brief but disastrous sea battle. Bonnet's lack of experience as both a pirate and a sea captain became obvious, and in the ensuing battle, half of his crew were killed, while the remainder were forced to flee. What remained of Bonnet's crew accompanied him to the Bahamas—where his life took yet another unusual twist.

In the island's capital, Nassau, Bonnet had a chance meeting with the infamous pirate Blackbeard. Bonnet had been injured in the battle off Florida, and being unable to captain his ship as well as he might as a result, he handed control of the *Revenge* and his remaining crew to Blackbeard. Together, the pair continued to plunder and capture ships for the remainder of the year, before going their separate ways in December 1717.

Bonnet's extraordinary story came to an end the following summer. Having spent the remainder of 1717 and early 1718 plundering and attacking ships all along America's east coast, in the summer of 1718, he was captured by the authorities in South Carolina and arrested. Charged with piracy, he was hanged the following December. The life of one of the age of piracy's most extraordinary characters was over.

## THE PIRATE WHO MET THE QUEEN OF ENGLAND

It's easy to think of pirates as all being men, but at least one of the most famous pirates of all time was, in fact, a woman.

Grace O'Malley was born in Ireland's County Mayo in 1530. Her father was a local Irish Gaelic chieftain named Owen

O'Malley—but as a pirate and privateer in his own right, he went by the name "Dubhdara," meaning Black Oak. While still a young woman, Grace joined her family on plundering and piracy missions all along Ireland's west coast.

As her experience on the wild seas of the Atlantic Ocean grew, so too did Grace's bravery. Before long, she, her family, and their fleet of ships were reportedly attacking vessels across a huge area of western Europe, from the islands of Scotland in the far north to the coast of Spain in the south.

Part of Grace O'Malley's success is that as well as pirating and attacking ships, she also opened trade routes and ferried much-needed supplies from mainland Europe into her family's lands in Ireland. Before long, she had a flourishing business empire, as well as a long-running reputation as a pirate.

One of the most extraordinary events of O'Malley's life, however, took place in the late 1500s, after much of Ireland had been conquered by England's Tudor monarchy. O'Malley and her family were forced from their land, one of her sons was killed in battle against the English, and another was arrested by the new Tudor governor of Ireland's Connaught region, Sir Richard Bingham. In response, O'Malley embarked on perhaps the most dangerous of all her sea missions. She set sail from Ireland, around the southern coast of England, and into the River Thames at London to seek an audience with Queen Elizabeth I herself.

Incredibly, the queen granted Grace's request to meet with her, and the two immensely powerful women sat down with one another in Greenwich. The pair talked for quite some time, with the queen eventually proving impressed enough by the pirate's extraordinary efforts to ensure her son was released from prison.

O'Malley later returned to Ireland, and after a remarkable seafaring and pirating life, she died in 1603 at the age of 73.

## BENJAMIN HORNIGOLD, KING OF PIRATES

One of the most famous pirates who ever lived, Captain Benjamin Hornigold, was born in England sometime around 1680.

An experienced sailor, Hornigold for a time even served the British government as a privateer in Europe and the Atlantic, chasing down rival Spanish and Portuguese vessels and plundering them in the name of the colonial crown. But by the early 1700s, he had relocated to the Caribbean, and there he started a long career in piracy.

From a base in the Bahamas, Hornigold operated across the Caribbean and the American east coast, attacking ships, stealing precious cargo, and earning himself a reputation as the local "King of Pirates."

By 1717, he had amassed a huge fleet of captured ships. He had so many, in fact, that it became necessary for him to name a second-in-command who could work alongside him as co-captain. The man Hornigold chose was an English sailor named Edward Teach—better known to history as Blackbeard!

For months, Hornigold and Blackbeard continued to chase down and plunder ships all across the Atlantic and Caribbean, concentrating their attacks along busy trade routes linking Cuba and Bermuda to the North American coast. But then, in the autumn of 1717, Hornigold had a sudden change of heart.

By this time, pirates had been disrupting England's sea trade for many years, and the king, George I, was determined to stamp it out. He appointed a new governor in the Caribbean and, through him, declared a new rule. The rule was: any pirate willing to hand himself in and cease his plundering would be granted a royal pardon, freeing him from any prospect of ever being punished or imprisoned (or worse, executed!) for his crimes. The offer proved too tempting for Hornigold, who handed himself in and ended his life at sea—at least, that is, for a little while!

Hornigold's long experience as a sailor, as well as the contacts he had in pirate-friendly ports and islands like the Bahamas, did not go unnoticed by the new Caribbean governors. They offered him a second deal. He was to be hired as a new pirate hunter who would use his experience and contacts to track down pirates who had not accepted the king's pardon and arrest them. For the next two years, the former "King of Pirates" did just that, turning his back on his former life as a pirate to become a pirate-chaser instead.

Sadly, Hornigold's time in service of the crown came to an end when, in the hurricane season of 1719, his ship was wrecked on a reef, and he drowned. He is believed to have been only 39 years old at the time of his death.

## THE ROBIN HOOD OF THE SEAS

Sam Bellamy was born in Devon, in the southwest corner of England, in 1689. Having worked all his life at sea, in his twenties, Bellamy crossed the Atlantic to seek his fame and fortune in America, relocating to Cape Cod in Massachusetts.

Bellamy quickly fell into piracy in the Americas and joined the crew of a ship called *Marianne*, alongside Benjamin Hornigold and Blackbeard. Before long, however, Bellamy—now known as "Black Sam" or "Captain Sam"—fell out with Hornigold and Blackbeard and rebelled against them. After they were ousted from control of the *Marianne*, he took control of the ship and embarked on a brief two-year career as a pirate in his own right.

From 1715 to 1717, Bellamy commandeered over 50 different ships off the waters of America's east coast, becoming one of the most successful and respected pirates of the day. He thought of himself as a "Robin Hood of the Seas," stealing only from the wealthiest merchants and sailors and distributing his haul among his crew. His most prized possession was a gigantic three-masted slave ship, the *Whydah*, which he and his crew captured off the coast of Cuba. On board was the equivalent of more than $5 million worth of gold and silver.

The *Whydah* quickly became Bellamy's flagship, and he continued to use it in raids along the Atlantic coast. Unfortunately, however, in April 1717, the *Whydah* was lost in an intense Atlantic storm. Bellamy—along with all but two of his crew—drowned.

And that was the end of the life of the wealthiest pirate in history.

## JACK AND ANNE, THE FIRST COUPLE OF PIRACY

While Grace O'Malley might have ruled the seas as an unexpected pirate queen in the 1500s, another Irishwoman, Anne Bonny, likewise earned a fearsome reputation as a pirate and part of an 18th-century power couple.

Although very little is known of Anne's early life, it is believed that she was born in Ireland before moving to America with her family as a child. The rest of her childhood was spent in the Carolinas, where she met and married a sailor-turned-pirate named James Bonny.

Together, the new husband and wife left the American mainland for the Bahamas, seeking to find fame and fortune as pirates in the Caribbean. James' career as a pirate did not last long, however.

Just like Benjamin Hornigold before him, when King George I's proposal to pardon any pirate willing to cease their plundering was announced shortly after the couple arrived in the Bahamas, James quickly returned to his life as an ordinary sailor and began working for the local governor. Anne, however, was determined to see her dream life as a pirate become a reality, and she soon grew unhappy with her husband's decision. Eventually, a chance meeting in a local bar with another pirate, nicknamed Calico Jack, proved a turning point. Anne abandoned James, stole a ship with Jack, and ran away with him back to sea!

The couple's life at sea, however, was short-lived. In 1720, after a run-in with the authorities, Jack and Anne were captured by pirate hunters in Jamaica. Jack was executed for piracy just a few weeks later, but Anne's fate is not known. Although she is believed to have told a court in Jamaica that she was pregnant, and so likely escaped the death penalty, there is no record of her release from jail, nor of her giving birth. Precisely what happened to Anne Bonny after her capture remains a complete mystery.

## DID YOU KNOW?

○ Pirates didn't all speak with the kind of accent you hear in movies! We only think that they did because that accent was popularized in movie adaptations of pirate stories!

○ Pirates didn't always wear eye patches because they were missing an eye. Some historians believe they were worn so that when pirates went below deck, they could remove the patch and the eye would be accustomed to the darkness, allowing them to see better in the dark hold!

○ The "pieces of eight" that pirates often mention in stories and films were actually gold coins used by the Spanish Empire.

○ The grandfather of the infamous pirate Blackbeard was a clergyman in rural Gloucestershire in the southwest of England.

○ The word "avast"—as in "Avast, me hearties!"—is an old naval command meaning "stop!"

○ Pirate's grog, a drink once popular among sailors, was a mixture of rum and water, sometimes sweetened with sugar and spices.

○ Ching Shih was a female pirate who is believed to have commanded a fleet of over 300 ships and 40,000 men!

○ Mary Read disguised herself as a man to become a pirate and was only discovered to be a woman at sea.

○ The earliest historical record of a pirate dates from almost 3,500 years ago.

○ The pirates' "Jolly Roger" flag, which features a skull and crossbones, was properly called the "Death's Head" flag.

# CHAPTER 5:
# KINGS & QUEENS

# HENRY VIII'S WRESTLING MATCH

If you had to name something for which England's great king Henry VIII is known, you would probably say his six wives. Perhaps, too, you might mention his war against the church and the great divide from the Catholic Church that Henry oversaw to ensure he could have a divorce. One thing you might not mention, however, is the time Henry challenged the king of France to a wrestling match!

The bout took place during an enormously extravagant royal summit held in Balinghem, in northern France, in 1520. Known as "The Field of the Cloth of Gold," the summit was intended to celebrate a newfound alliance between Henry VIII and France's young king, Francis I. Both kings were in their twenties, and both were in control of immensely powerful countries. The summit was arranged so the two could set aside their nations' historical differences and instead join forces to present a strong united front to the rest of Europe.

The Cloth of Gold was an extraordinarily lavish occasion that was so grand it threatened to bankrupt both countries. Huge banquet halls were decorated and played host to immense feasts where guests could drink from fountains full of wine. Makeshift temporary palaces were erected in which the guests could all be housed. Hundreds of livestock—including 3,000 sheep and 800 calves—were brought from England to France to keep the royal parties well fed throughout the week-long event.

Far more than just a political meeting, the Cloth of Gold quickly became an immense celebration of England and France's collaboration. The centerpiece was a grand sporting competition, which the two young kings were both more than keen to get involved with themselves.

Not only were both Henry and Francis of similar age but they were also equally matched in height and weight, were both expert horsemen and hunters, and were both in physically impressive shape. Sensing that he had met his athletic match, Henry reportedly suggested that the two take part in a wrestling match to find out once and for all who was the stronger and more athletic of the pair.

Unfortunately for him, however, it was Francis who was victorious!

## THE KING WHO THOUGHT HE WAS MADE OF GLASS

Many kings and queens throughout history have suffered bouts of ill health or endured terrible illnesses or conditions throughout their lives. The infamous English king Richard III, for instance, is believed to have had a condition that affected the shape and growth of his spine. It was a disability Shakespeare was all too keen to take advantage of in his play *Richard III*, in which the king is portrayed as a villainous hunchback!

Of all the royal illnesses of the past, however, perhaps the most bizarre was a form of madness that afflicted a medieval king of France.

Charles VI was crowned king of France in 1380 at the age of just 11. Given his young age, for the first ten years of Charles' reign, he was supported by his uncles and extended family. They acted as advisors to ensure he ruled over his kingdom as wisely and responsibly as possible. When he turned 21, however, Charles' panel of family advisors was disbanded, and he was left to rule alone.

The first years of Charles' reign were largely successive, and to the people of France, he became known as Charles the Beloved. In his mid-twenties, however, the king began to experience bouts of madness. He would wildly attack people, disappear into deep depressions, and even forget that he was the king at all! As his mental health worsened, however, Charles came to believe an extraordinary delusion that plagued him for the remainder of his life. Bizarrely, the king became absolutely convinced that his body was made of glass.

Any sudden movement, the king believed, would cause his body to shatter into thousands of tiny shards. His bones, he thought, were like rods of glass that could be broken with only the slightest pressure or knocks. To counteract his apparent brittleness, the king had iron rods sewn into his clothing to avoid his arms and legs being bent or bumped or breaking to pieces if he fell over. He would spend his days swaddled in blankets to protect himself. When seated, he would demand his lower body be wrapped in cushions and coverlets to avoid his backside shattering!

Eventually, Charles' condition proved too much. "His malady grew worse every day," the pope Pius II wrote of the king, "until his mind was completely gone." Having never recovered from his madness, Charles died in 1422, at the age of 53.

## THE KING OF ENGLAND'S PET POLAR BEAR

Queen Elizabeth II, famously, kept a number of pet corgi dogs throughout her life. The medieval king Henry III of England, however, had a rather more unusual—and rather more sizable!—pet that was given to him by his friend, the king of Norway.

Although today it is a museum, England's famous Tower of London has served many purposes over its long history, including a prison, a royal mint for producing coins, a storehouse for arms and weaponry, and even a giant menagerie filled with exotic animals. Over the years, this menagerie housed everything from elephants to lions—but in 1251, Henry III was forced to add an especially remarkable animal to the royal collection in the Tower when King Haakon IV of Norway gifted him a pet polar bear!

The "white bear," as it was known, soon proved a popular sight in the city. Its handlers would take it down to the nearby River Thames every morning to swim and catch fish.

The streets around the Tower were lined with onlookers keen to catch sight of the king's extraordinary pet. A muzzle and chains were especially made to allow the bear to be walked safely through the crowded streets—although to be on the safe side, traffic on the roads around the Tower was halted whenever the bear was taken out of its enclosure!

The bear was so popular both with the king and the people of London that in 1253, a royal decree was issued in which the king—worried that his bear was not being looked after sufficiently—set aside six pence per day (equivalent to more than £70, or around $100 today!) to pay for its upkeep.

Today, a statue of the bear remains on display at the Tower of London, celebrating perhaps the most unusual resident in its long history!

## QUEEN VICTORIA, THE GRANDMOTHER OF EUROPE

Until she was overtaken by Elizabeth II in the 21st century, England's Queen Victoria was the longest-reigning monarch in royal history. Having taken the throne in 1837 at the age of just 18, following the death of her uncle and the previous king William IV, Victoria went on to reign as queen of the United Kingdom for the next 63 years until her death in 1901 at the age of 81.

During her time on the throne, in 1840, the queen married her consort, Prince Albert, and the couple went on to have nine children. They, in turn, went on to marry into other royal houses from all across Europe and had families of their own—and as such, England's Queen Victoria went on to become grandmother to an entire generation of European royalty, earning her the nickname "The Grandmother of Europe."

The queen's eldest son, Edward, for instance (who went on to become the English king Edward VII) married Princess Alexandra of Denmark. Her second-eldest son, Alfred, married a Russian duchess. Her other sons, Arthur and Leopold, married into the royal families of Prussia and Waldeck (a German dukedom). Her daughters, Alice, Helena, and Beatrice, all likewise married German and Austrian dukes, while her daughter Princess Louise married the Duke of Argyll, from Scotland.

Perhaps most remarkable of all, however, was the fact that Victoria's eldest daughter, the Princess Royal (who was also named Victoria), married into the German royal family and became the queen of Frederick of Prussia. Their son Wilhelm, in turn, eventually became the emperor of Germany, so that when World War I broke out in 1914, the kings of both England and Germany—who would find themselves on opposite sides during the war—were both grandchildren of Queen Victoria!

# THE HIDDEN TALENTS OF BRITAIN'S LONGEST-REIGNING QUEEN

Queen Victoria might have ruled for 63 years, but her great-great-granddaughter Elizabeth II eventually overtook her record, ruling for a total of 70 years, from 1952 until her death in 2022 at the age of 96.

As Britain's longest-reigning monarch—and one of the longest-reigning monarchs in world history, for that matter—Queen Elizabeth II oversaw a dramatic period of change. During her seven decades on the throne, the world became a very different place. As a result, she earned herself a place in history books for a number of remarkable firsts achieved during her reign.

Her coronation in 1953, for instance, was the first to be broadcast on television. In 1976, she became the first monarch in history to send an email and, in 2003, the first monarch to sit for a hologram portrait. And when the Royal Family set up a Twitter account (now social media platform X) in 2014, she became the first royal to send a tweet.

But besides the remarkable firsts and achievements of her reign, Elizabeth II led such an extraordinary life that she also had a number of hidden talents, some of which only came to light to a modern audience after her death.

During World War II, for instance, the future queen—then merely 19-year-old Princess Elizabeth, the eldest daughter of the wartime king George VI—decided to do her bit for the war effort. She enlisted in the services and trained as a truck mechanic. In doing so, she not only learned how to fix motor vehicle engines but also became the first female member of the royal family to serve in the military.

Elizabeth II also learned to speak fluent French, and during official state visits to France, Canada, and other French-speaking nations, she often talked with other leaders and citizens using their own language. The queen spoke the language fluently because, in childhood, several of her royal nannies and governesses had been French and Belgian, and she had picked up the language from them!

Perhaps strangest of all, however, is that the late queen even went to the moon—without ever leaving Earth! When plans were being made for the Apollo 11 moon landings in 1969, NASA approached world leaders from more than 70 different countries, asking them to record messages recognizing the remarkable feat of human achievement that was about to take place. The queen was among the dozens of leaders who responded and recorded a message of congratulations that was then recorded on microfilm and deposited on the lunar surface by Neil Armstrong. She said: "On behalf of the British people, I salute the skills and courage which have brought man to the moon. May this endeavor increase the knowledge and well-being of mankind." The messages remain in a metal container on the moon to this day!

# DID YOU KNOW?

○ Due to a centuries-old law, all wild mute swans in the United Kingdom are technically owned by the king.

○ At the time of his death, Henry VIII's waistline measured 54 inches!

○ Historical and medical records claim that James I of England had such an unusually large tongue that it appeared too big for his mouth and left him suffering from a speech impediment.

○ British king William IV was nicknamed "Silly Billy."

○ Jane Seymour, the third wife of Henry VIII, gave him the son he so desperately wanted. As a result, she is the only wife buried alongside him in Windsor.

○ England's crown jewels were stolen during the reign of Charles II. The king was reportedly so impressed by the cleverness and wit of the man who stole them that the thief escaped punishment!

○ When Henry I died in 1135, his internal organs were removed and buried in France. The rest of his body was buried in England.

○ Louis XIV of France ruled for 72 years.

○ The famous Russian tsar Peter the Great did not like to hire executioners and preferred to execute his prisoners himself!

○ Russian queen Empress Elizabeth once tried to dye her hair, but the dye was so poor that she was forced to shave her head. Rather than wear a wig, the empress demanded that all the other women in her court shave their heads too!

# CHAPTER 6:
# FAKERS & FORGERS

# THE MAN WHO SOLD THE STATUE OF LIBERTY

George Parker was born in New York in 1860 and later became one of the most unusual con men in American history.

We don't know an awful lot about his childhood, other than that his family immigrated to America from Ireland. They had arrived in New York at a point when the city was a huge melting pot of people coming to the United States from all over the world, hoping to make a better life for themselves. And although Parker was one of them, he decided to make these new arrivals the victims of a bizarre swindling scheme.

Parker's con first came about in the 1880s. The idea behind it was simple: posing as a real estate agent, dressed in a smart suit and hat, he would approach someone who had only just arrived in New York and convince them that he was the owner of one of the city's most famous landmarks—from the Brooklyn Bridge to the Statue of Liberty. As the pair talked, Parker would gradually make it known to his victim that he was offering the landmark for sale and would then sell it to them for thousands of dollars.

Part of Parker's con involved convincing his unsuspecting buyer that what he was selling them would earn them more than their money back. The Statue of Liberty, he would say, could be opened to tourists who would pay the new owner for tickets to visit it. The new owner of the Brooklyn Bridge—which Parker sold on more than one occasion, to multiple different victims!—would be able to line it with toll booths and charge people for crossing it. No matter how much the buyer had to pay, Parker would say they would make that money back (and much, much more!) very quickly.

As well as the Brooklyn Bridge and the Statue of Liberty, Parker also managed to "sell" the likes of Madison Square Garden, Ulysses S. Grant's tomb, and the Metropolitan Museum of Art, as well as dozens of empty lots and warehouses across the city. In truth, of course, Parker did not own any of these, but that did not stop him from conducting his con several times a week for years—earning hundreds of thousands of dollars in the process!

Parker understandably ended up in court on numerous occasions, charged with fraud. But somehow, he would always end up back out on the street, carrying out his con again and again. There is even a story that as he left court one day, he asked to be handed his coat and hat—then promptly walked out of the courthouse wearing the sheriff's jacket!

In 1928, however, Parker's crime spree had gone on so long that the judge was forced to hand down a life sentence, and he was taken away to New York's famous Sing Sing Prison. He died there in 1936—apparently having befriended most of his prison guards and becoming one of the jailhouse's most popular inmates!

# PERKIN WARBECK, PRETENDER TO THE THRONE

Way back in 1491, a man named Perkin Warbeck arrived in Ireland from Europe. He had been born into a wealthy family in Flanders, a region of Belgium, and had grown up working for various merchants and businesses all over the continent.

His work now brought him to Cork, where his wealth, extravagant clothes, and unusual accent soon made him stick out from the crowd. The local Irish people presumed, mistakenly, that Warbeck must be of royal descent—but rather than correct them, Warbeck and his companions decided to go along with it!

At that time, England was being ruled by the Tudors—the grand royal family that would eventually include the likes of Henry VIII and Elizabeth I. Unlike England, however, Ireland had traditionally been a supporter of the Tudors' rivals, the House of York, against whom the Tudors had just won a long war.

The local Irish people wrongly presumed that Perkin Warbeck must be the Duke of York—the House of York's heir to the English throne, who would have become king if York had won the war. As a result, they began rallying their forces, determined to throw the Tudors from power and install Warbeck in their place.

Seeing this as an opportunity to steal the English crown for himself, Warbeck went along with the mistake. Pretending to be the Duke of York, he began bringing together an army of troops from his home in Europe to support his claim to the throne. Eventually, he had an army of around 6,000 troops and supporters—pulled together from Ireland, Scotland, France, Austria, Spain, and the Netherlands—and in 1496 launched an invasion of northern England from Scotland.

Unfortunately, the plan failed as quickly as it had begun. The Scottish king, James IV, had believed that the north of England would welcome the Duke of York's return and that the people there would join up with Perkin's attack on the Tudors. Instead, there was a huge amount of resistance, and he was only able to move a few miles over the border— destroying a handful of farms and buildings in the process— before a local army pushed the invaders back into Scotland.

Warbeck, however, was determined to try again. In 1497, he invaded England once more, this time from the sea. Landing in Cornwall, a county in the far southwest corner of England, he and his supporters quickly began marching across the English countryside, heading toward London. But again, they were quickly stopped in their tracks by the king's armies, and Warbeck was captured and sent to the Tower of London where he was executed in 1499.

# MARY TOFT, THE WOMAN WHO GAVE BIRTH TO RABBITS

One of the strangest hoaxes in history was carried out by a woman named Mary Toft way back in 1726.

Toft was born in Godalming, a town around 30 miles outside London, in 1703. In her early twenties, Toft claimed that she had become pregnant—but when she gave birth, instead of a baby, she produced a litter of rabbits!

As if that were not bizarre enough, Toft seemingly didn't stop producing animals. She would go to bed in the evening and wake to find random animals in her bed that she had supposedly given birth to overnight.

Understandably, her case soon came to the attention of a local doctor who, in turn, passed it on to a famous surgeon in London named Nathaniel St. André, the king's own royal doctor. When he went to Surrey to investigate the case, St. André found Toft in bed at the local doctor's house; to his surprise, while he was there, she apparently gave birth to another litter of rabbits.

Fascinated by Toft's case, St. André took some of the rabbits back to London and told the king the remarkable story. Before long, Toft was a national celebrity.

Although both St. André and Toft's own doctor were convinced her case was true, there were many others who were not. To silence his critics, St. André arranged for Mary to be brought to London, where she was met by a huge crowd of curious onlookers and physicians from all over Europe. She was taken to a house in Leicester Square, where she remained for several days, seemingly going into labor time and again. But oddly (and to St. André's annoyance!) she never once produced any rabbits.

A few days after her arrival in London, however, a porter working at the house where Mary was staying was caught trying to smuggle a rabbit into her bedroom. This was all the proof that was needed to uncover the hoax, to which Mary eventually confessed. She was later imprisoned as a fraud— while the doctors who had believed her case to be genuine were left very embarrassed!

## GREGOR MACGREGOR, THE ISLAND-SELLING SWINDLER

One of the wildest swindles in history was that of a Scottish adventurer named Gregor MacGregor.

Born in Stirlingshire, Scotland, in 1786, as a young man MacGregor served in the British Army. He fought in battles and wars all over the world. Much of his military career was spent in South America and the Caribbean, and it was his experiences here that gave him the idea for his scam.

MacGregor returned to Scotland from the Caribbean in 1821, full of wild stories about his time away. He claimed that while in Central America, he had met with King George Frederic Augustus, the ruler of the Mosquito Coast (a region in modern-day Nicaragua). Apparently, the king had made MacGregor the "Cazique of Poyais"—a prince of the lush island nation of Poyais.

The country, MacGregor explained, was so lush and tropical that corn could be harvested all throughout the year, producing three times the amount of food that land in Europe could produce. The rivers there were lined with nuggets of gold, MacGregor said, and the water that flowed in them was so pure and clear that it could quench anyone's thirst in an instant. The forests around them, MacGregor went on, were filled with wild animals that could be easily hunted for their delicious meat, while even the trees themselves were so heavy with fruit that their branches almost bent down to the ground!

The picture MacGregor painted of the island seemed too good to be true—for the very good reason that it was!

In fact, there was no island of Poyais, and MacGregor had not been appointed prince of a Caribbean paradise by the king of the Mosquito Coast. The entire story was a scam, which MacGregor had concocted as a way of making money.

Producing maps, charts, official-looking documents, and even a fake flag of Poyais, MacGregor managed to convince many wealthy merchants and aristocrats to invest their money in his fake island. He took out two enormous £200,000 loans (equivalent to more than £18 million/$22 million today!) based on the value of the land and used the cash to win himself a place in English high society. Soon, he was selling hundreds of acres of fake tropical land to the wealthiest people in England.

Eventually, however, MacGregor's scheme began to unravel. Some of those who had invested in MacGregor's scheme traveled to the Mosquito Coast themselves, only to find that no such island of Poyais existed. When word of the deception reached England in 1823, MacGregor fled to France—and there began the scheme all over again!

After several more years of taking out loans on land that didn't exist and selling acres of territory in a fake country, people again became suspicious of MacGregor's dealings, and he was arrested. After a brief trial, he escaped justice once again and fled Europe for the Americas.

He saw out the rest of his days living in luxury in tropical Venezuela!

## MARY CARLETON, THE FAKE GERMAN PRINCESS

In 1642, a lady named Mary Moders was born in the ancient English city of Canterbury.

At some point during her time there, Mary married a local shoemaker named Thomas Stedman. A few years later, she abandoned her life in Canterbury and relocated to nearby Dover, where she wed another man named Thomas Day.

Being married to more than one person at the same time was a crime, and Mary's double life soon brought her to the attention of the authorities, and she was arrested. Somehow managing to escape punishment, she fled to Europe—and within a matter of years, was engaged to marry a third man, this time in the German city of Cologne.

By now, it was the early 1660s, and Mary—still barely 20 years old—was already making plans for her third wedding. As her German fiancé began pushing her to make the final arrangements for their big day, however, Mary once again fled (taking all her wedding presents and her husband's money with her) and returned to England.

This time, Mary decided to use her experiences in Germany to her advantage. She moved to London and there began telling everyone that she was a princess and the orphaned daughter of a German nobleman, and she had been forced to flee to England to escape a bad marriage. Her story worked, and Mary was welcomed into London's high society—where she promptly met and married a fourth man, a wealthy surgeon named John Carleton.

In 1663, however, a mysterious anonymous letter exposed Mary's web of lies, and she was arrested. Her case understandably became the talk of the city, and Mary began adding to her already extraordinary story to take full advantage of the publicity.

John Carleton, Mary now claimed, was the real villain of her tale. She said he had pretended to be an English lord and charmed Mary into their marriage in an attempt to steal her (now rather large!) fortune. This story, too, of course, was a complete lie—but it nevertheless proved convincing enough for Mary to escape punishment.

Mary continued to make the most of her newfound fame, even producing and performing in a play on the London stage that told the story of her life. According to some accounts, she even married another man—one of her admirers, whom she met after her show—only to go on to leave him, too, and take all of his cash in the process!

Over the years that followed, Mary continued to use a string of fake sob stories and identities to woo rich men and then steal their fortunes. She wed one man while again pretending to be a rich heiress fleeing an unsuitable husband. She convinced another man that she was destined to inherit her family's vast fortune, but only if she married. When he fell for this deceitful story, Mary again fled with all his money midway through preparing their wedding day.

Even after Mary's crimes caught up with her, she did not stop. In 1671, she was found guilty of stealing a silver tankard and transported to one of England's colonial prisons in Jamaica. Within a year, she had invented another fake story for herself that allowed her to escape, gain free passage back to England, and pass herself off once again as a rich heiress. And yet again, the story worked: in 1672,

Mary wed another London merchant—before making off with all his money!

Eventually, however, Mary's long crime spree came to an end. Shortly after her final marriage, in December 1672, a London jailer recognized Mary and turned her in to the authorities. At that time, returning from transportation abroad was a capital offense, and so Mary—aged just 30 at the time—was sentenced to be hanged.

The life of one of the boldest and most madcap fakers in history was over.

## DID YOU KNOW?

- In 2024, people lost $17 billion to online scams in the United States alone.
- The Con Queen of California was the name given to a notorious swindler in Hollywood who would hire people to work on fake movies, take their money to fund the movie, and then disappear.
- One of the writers on the '70s sitcom The Love Boat once tried to sell a fake interview with the author J.D. Salinger to People magazine. Salinger ended up suing him, saying they had never even met!
- In the 1930s, an American conman in France named Count Victor Lustig successfully "sold" the Eiffel Tower in an elaborate money-making scam.

- Lustig later explained some of the rules of what made a good conman: "Never be untidy," "Never boast," and "Never get drunk."
- An Indian conman named Mithilesh Kumar Srivastava also managed to "sell" the Taj Mahal, along with many other monuments across India...
- ...and went on to be imprisoned for fraud—but escaped from jail ten times!
- William Chaloner was a serial conman in 17th-century England. He was eventually discovered by the scientist Sir Isaac Newton!
- In 1859, Percy Redwood, a sheep farmer in New Zealand, married a rich local woman named Agnes Ottaway, despite her family's suspicions. After the wedding, it was discovered that not only was Redwood heavily in debt and the romance was a scam to swindle money from Ottaway but "he" was, in fact, a female con artist named Amy Bock, who had disguised herself as a man!
- The average amount of money lost in a scam today is $545.

# CHAPTER 7:
# EXPLORERS & ADVENTURERS

# CAPTAIN COOK'S AROUND-THE-WORLD TRIPS

One of the greatest achievements in the history of exploration is a feat known as circumnavigation—a journey that goes all the way around the entire world.

The first successful circumnavigation of the Earth took place in 1519 under the leadership of the great Portuguese explorer Ferdinand Magellan. He and his crew of around 250 men set sail from Spain aboard five ships in September 1519, seeking a western route to the East Indies—the islands we now know as the Philippines, Indonesia, and their neighboring island nations.

By winter 1520, they had reached the southern tip of South America by discovering a western route into the Pacific Ocean, now known as the Strait of Magellan. They sailed on to arrive in the East Indies in 1521.

Magellan himself, however, was killed in fighting in the Philippines in April 1521, and a series of storms, mutinies, and outbreaks of scurvy destroyed four of the fleet's ships and claimed the lives of over 200 of its men. By the time the single surviving ship, the *Victoria*, returned to Spain in September 1522, fewer than 20 men—now captained by the ship's navigator, Juan Sebastián Elcano—remained to finish the trip.

Clearly, completing such a long and difficult journey was far from straightforward all those years ago. Yet around two centuries after Ferdinand Magellan set sail, another famous explorer successfully managed to complete not just one circumnavigation of the Earth, but three!

James Cook was a British explorer who was born in Yorkshire, in northern England, in 1728. Having worked as an apprentice to a shipbuilder in his childhood, Cook joined the Royal Navy in 1752 and over the next 15 years became one of Britain's most accomplished and experienced naval officers. Cook's work at sea took him all over the world, both on voyages of discovery and in naval warfare. As a result, when the British Royal Society—a scientific society aimed at learning more about the world—began planning a round-the-world voyage of exploration, Cook seemed like the perfect person to captain it.

Cook and his mixed crew of sailors and scientists set sail from England in the summer of 1768, heading south down the Atlantic Ocean to the tip of South America, and across the Pacific Ocean to Tahiti. From there, Cook sailed onwards to New Zealand and Australia, then home across the Indian Ocean, around the southernmost tip of Africa, and then northwards, back up the Atlantic, to arrive in England in March 1771.

The voyage had taken a little under three years, but it had been an immense success. The scientists on board had recorded a huge amount of new data about the world, the moon, the stars, and navigation—while Cook himself had become the first person in history to sail all the way around New Zealand, chart the coastline of Australia, and safely sail by the Great Barrier Reef. As a result, just over a year after he returned to England, Cook was asked to captain another round-the-world sea journey, this time even more daring than the last.

Cook's second voyage set sail in the summer of 1772, on board two ships, the *Resolution* and the *Adventure*. This time, he headed eastwards, down the coast of Africa. The aim was to travel as far south as possible to see if he could reach Antarctica and discover the legendary continent of *Terra Australis*—a gigantic, fabled landmass believed to exist somewhere in the Southern or Pacific Ocean.

This second voyage made Cook the first explorer in history to cross the Antarctic Circle, but the conditions there prevented him from heading any further southward. He was forced to continue on to the Pacific, having not reached Antarctica itself.

Once in the Pacific, Cook again visited New Zealand, and from there Tonga, Tahiti, and Easter Island. Having found nothing but these smaller, isolated tropical islands in the Pacific Ocean, Cook successfully proved that Terra Australis was nothing more than a myth; having rounded the tip of South America, he headed home and arrived back in England in July 1775. But he was not done yet.

A year later, in the summer of 1776, Cook set sail again, this time charged with finding a northern route—either across the top of Russia or Alaska and Canada—linking the Atlantic and Pacific Oceans. Just like last time, Cook's third voyage headed east, down the coast of Africa and into the Indian Ocean, from where he sailed on past the south coast of Australia and into the Pacific.

Once there, Cook continued northwards, heading up the Pacific Ocean from New Zealand, seeking a route back to the Atlantic. Midway through his third Pacific journey, however, disaster struck: in Hawaii, an argument with the local Hawaiian people led to a brief fight in which Cook was killed. His crew was ultimately forced to continue his final voyage without him, sailing on from Hawaii, around the northern Pacific, before giving up their search for a northern passage back to the Atlantic Ocean and heading home to England via South America.

Although Cook might not have completed his third circumnavigation, the crew and the ship on which he set sail, at least, did. His contribution to our knowledge of the world, its geography, and our way around it, meanwhile, is one of the greatest in the history of exploration.

## THE MAN WHO GAVE US POTATOES

They're one of the most widely eaten vegetables in the world, used in everything from fast-food fries and packets of chips to the richest of dishes in the most lavish of restaurants. But did you know that our fondness for the humble potato can be traced back to just one man?

Despite being widely grown throughout America and Europe, the potato is actually native to South America. The first people to grow them in any great numbers were, in fact, the ancient Incas of the Andes Mountains in Peru, who are believed to have begun farming and cultivating potatoes as many as 1,800 years ago.

Then, around 500 years ago, explorers from Spain, known as *conquistadors*, began arriving in Central and South America, looking to establish new colonies and claim the land there for the Spanish crown. On their arrival in the Andes, these conquistadors became the first Europeans to try a potato, and they took a supply of the vegetable back to Spain.

At first, however, the Europeans were not particularly keen on this newly imported vegetable. Unsure of how best to prepare it, they also struggled to grow it. The long, hot summers and cold, dark winters of southern Europe were a lot different from the sunnier, cooler, wetter summers of the high Andes, and the plants struggled to grow. Those that did produce potatoes of any usable size, meanwhile, typically did so late in the year—so late that they were quickly killed off by heavy rain and early frosts.

In the late 1500s, however, things began to change. In 1588, the English explorer Sir Walter Raleigh—a close friend and member of the court of Queen Elizabeth I—was given a house in southern Ireland, in the town of Youghal, near Cork. And there he is said to have planted a potato plant, which quickly thrived in the rich, damp soil and coastal Atlantic climate. Farmers in the area soon began to grow the crop themselves, producing larger, hardier, and fast-growing varieties that quickly became one of Ireland's most widely grown and used staple foods. And from there, the potato quickly caught on across Britain and the rest of the Western world.

One question remains, though: where did Raleigh himself get his hands on a potato plant?

One theory claims that Raleigh, like the Spanish conquistadors before him, brought the plant back from one of his voyages to the New World. Another claims that he simply picked it up in Europe himself, from sellers and merchants in Spain keen to make the most of their newfound discovery. One story, however, claims that the plant was not Raleigh's at all and was in fact found by locals in Ireland among the cargo of a Spanish ship lost off the coast (perhaps in the aftermath of Spain's failed invasion of Elizabethan England, the Spanish Armada).

Whatever the truth may be, it is the age of exploration that took the potato out of the Andes for the very first time more than five centuries ago and set it on its course to become one of the world's most used vegetables.

## THE VIKINGS WHO VISITED AMERICA

If someone were to ask you who discovered America, you'd likely say it was Christopher Columbus.

It's certainly true that way back in 1492, Columbus set sail from Europe across the Atlantic Ocean, arriving in the so-called New World toward the end of the year. Although he wrongly believed that he had discovered a western route to Asia—mistaking Cuba for mainland China and the other islands of the Caribbean for the islands of the East Indies—what Columbus had actually done was become the first European to explore the Americas.

There's only one problem with this story, however: Columbus actually *wasn't* the first European to set foot in the Americas!

Almost 500 years before Columbus even set sail, seafaring Vikings are known to have traveled across the Atlantic Ocean to what is now Greenland and Canada, making *them* the first Europeans to land on American soil.

Historical records show that the Vikings at least knew about Greenland—the vast arctic island to the northeast of northern Canada—from around the 9th century onwards. A Viking explorer and seafarer named Gunnbjörn Ulfsson was blown far off course while attempting to sail from Norway to Iceland in the late 800s CE. In the process, he unexpectedly spotted the shores and islands off of Greenland.

Around a century later, an explorer named Erik Thorvaldsson, known as Erik the Red, led a group of Viking sailors to Greenland, where he founded a village sometime in the 980s CE. It was he who gave the island of Greenland its name.

Now in the high Arctic, the Vikings continued to explore the islands of northern North America. Around 1000 CE, Erik the Red's son, Leif Erikson, sailed from his father's settlements in Greenland and explored a region he called "Vinland." Although historians are not quite sure precisely where Erikson ended up, it is likely that he sailed as far south as Newfoundland and explored some of the mainland coast of Canada—and perhaps the eastern seaboard—in the process.

In fact, in 2021, some samples of wooden artifacts uncovered in Newfoundland that showed signs of having been cut by Viking tools were reliably dated to 1021 CE. This proved that the Vikings had at least reached modern-day Canada by this time—and so had arrived in North America at least 471 years before Christopher Columbus!

## "DR LIVINGSTONE, I PRESUME?"

Exploring can be a dangerous job, of course. Venturing into seas and lands that have never been explored before is understandably risky even today. In the past, however, long before we had mapped and connected the entire world with telephones and satellites, traveling somewhere with no way of easily returning or communicating with home took astonishing bravery. And one of the most remarkable stories of precisely that also has one of the most remarkable and unexpected endings.

Dr. Jonathan Livingstone was a Scottish explorer and Christian missionary who was born on the outskirts of Glasgow, in southern Scotland, in 1813. Having studied medicine, Livingstone decided to combine his interest in healing the sick with his interest in the church. He became a missionary doctor—a medical expert who travels to remote parts of the world to provide medical care and also spread the word of God.

Livingstone's work took him to Africa in the 1840s, and over the decades that followed, he embarked on several expeditions exploring enormous regions of the continent, following the river Zambezi in the south and the river Nile in the north. His explorations allowed geographers and navigators to map Africa in greater detail than ever before, and what he discovered vastly increased Western knowledge of African culture and wildlife.

Throughout his travels, Livingstone would keep in contact as best he could with his family and friends back home in England, writing letters that he would send from towns and cities whenever he could. In 1866, however, Livingstone embarked on what would be his very last journey to Africa—this time searching for the source of the river Nile—and seemingly disappeared. His letters home simply stopped, and for months, no word reached any of his friends or family to update them on his whereabouts. One of the most famous explorers of the 19th century had, it seemed, become lost somewhere in Africa.

As news of Livingstone's disappearance broke, people across the globe became increasingly interested in what had happened to him. As a result, in 1869—three years after Livingstone had set off to find the source of the Nile—a British journalist working for the *New York Herald* named Henry Morton Stanley set sail for Africa in an attempt to solve the case.

Stanley's letters and articles sent back to New York caused a sensation, as the *Herald's* readers followed his journey around Africa with enormous interest. In 1871, Stanley reported that he had arrived in Zanzibar, a tropical island off Africa's east coast, and from there was heading inland to Lake Tanganyika, where he had been told by locals that Livingstone had last been seen. Astonishingly, against all odds, on November 10, 1871, Stanley arrived in the town of Ujiji in Tanzania, and there on the shores of the lake, found...David Livingstone!

As the two men met for the first time, after almost three years of Stanley's search, Stanley uttered the now-famous greeting, "Dr. Livingstone, I presume?"

Livingstone, Stanley learned, had taken ill in Africa, but luckily Stanley had sufficient medicine to treat him, and he made a slow recovery over the weeks and months that followed. Eventually, he recovered enough to continue his hunt for the source of the Nile, but sadly, he took ill again and died in 1873.

As for Stanley, his reports of his successful search for Livingstone made him immensely famous. He used his fame—and his contacts in the press—to continue Livingstone's work exploring Africa and, like him, eventually went on to become one of the 19th century's most renowned explorers and adventurers.

## JOHN CABOT AND HIS "NEW-FOUND LAND"

When you think about it, the name "Newfoundland" is a pretty strange one! So who exactly gave this "new-found land" this rather unusual name?

John Cabot was a 15th-century European explorer. Born in Venice (and originally named Giovanni Caboto), Cabot eventually moved to England and there sought a career as a seafarer, explorer, and adventurer. Having moved to the port city of Bristol in the 1480s, Cabot set up a base for his exploration and from there used maps and charts to find—just like Columbus before him—what he believed was a route west to Asia.

After years of planning, in 1496, Cabot was finally given the royal seal of approval for his voyage across the Atlantic by King Henry VII, and the following year, he set sail from Bristol. Unfortunately—and again, just like Columbus before him!—Cabot failed to find a westward route to the Far East. Instead, he landed high up on the coast of North America, much further northwards than Columbus.

Although exactly where Cabot landed in North America is unclear, he named his discovery for precisely what it was: newly found land! From there, he continued to explore the eastern coast of what is now modern-day Canada, with much of his work used by England in the decades after his voyage to establish colonies on the American Atlantic.

## DID YOU KNOW?

○ America is named after an Italian explorer named Amerigo Vespucci.

○ The Silk Road—the long trade route used by Marco Polo between Europe and Asia—was more than 5,500 miles long!

○ Spanish sailors knew the English explorer Sir Francis Drake as "El Draque"—the dragon!

○ Christopher Columbus took not one but three ships with him to America, named the *Niña*, the *Pinta*, and the *Santa Maria*.

○ Columbus also made repeat journeys to America. After his first voyage in 1492, he returned in 1493, 1498, and 1502.

○ Marco Polo was nicknamed Il Milione, or "The Million," apparently because he liked to talk about the "millions" of things he saw on his travels.

○ Marco Polo came from a family of explorers: his parents and grandparents had all journeyed from Italy to the Middle East to lay down new trade routes.

- On a trip to Antarctica in the mid-1800s, the explorer James Clark Ross discovered the continent has volcanoes—and named one of the fiery peaks Mount Terror!
- The polar explorer Jules Dumont discovered tiny penguins in Antarctica, which he named after his wife Adele. The birds are still called Adelie penguins today!
- Peter Scott, son of the explorer Sir Robert Scott, founded the World Wildlife Fund.

# CHAPTER 8:
# BATTLES & WARS

# THE WAR THAT LASTED LESS THAN AN HOUR

The American Civil War lasted four years, from 1861 to 1865. So too did World War I, from 1914 to 1918, while World War II lasted almost six years, from 1939 to 1945.

Head even further back in time, though, and you'll find wars that lasted not just a few years, but a few decades. Despite its name, for instance, the famous Hundred Years War between England and France lasted a full 116 years, from 1337 to 1453!

In the late 19th century, however, there was a war that not only lasted less than a day—it actually lasted a little under an hour!

The war was fought on the island of Zanzibar, off the coast of modern-day Tanzania in East Africa. At the time, the island had its own local ruler, a sultan, but it remained under the strict colonial control of Great Britain.

On the one hand, the British were hoping to end slavery in Zanzibar and then use the island as a free base from which to set up new trade routes across the Indian Ocean. But on the other hand, the British also wanted to ensure they kept their strict control of the island and that the sultan of Zanzibar remained loyal to Britain's rule, with no real power of his own.

Understandably, not everyone on Zanzibar was happy with these rules, but for many years, sultan after sultan respected them, and so the British maintained their control of the island. In August 1896, however, the existing sultan of Zanzibar, Sayyid Hamad, suddenly died, and a new sultan who disliked the British, Prince Khalid, swept to power in his place.

Prince Khalid quickly took control of the sultan's palace and, knowing that the British would not be happy with him in control of the island, on August 26, he surrounded it with 3,000 soldiers so that he could defend himself against an attack. Sure enough, when news reached the British that Khalid had taken over Zanzibar, they gave him 24 hours to step down or else, at 9 a.m. the next day, they would be forced to attack.

Over the hours that followed, five Royal Navy warships were moved into the seas off Zanzibar, and the British readied hundreds of troops for an assault on the island. As promised, at 9 a.m. on August 27—with Khalid still in power and refusing to leave the palace—the ships began firing on the sultan's palace, which was soon in flames. Five hundred of Prince Khalid's soldiers were killed in just a matter of minutes, forcing the sultan to surrender at 9:40 a.m.

The entire Anglo-Zanzibar War, as it became known, had lasted just 37 minutes!

# THE STRAY DOG THAT STARTED A WAR

Throughout their long history, the two ancient countries of Greece and Bulgaria, in the far southeast corner of Europe, have gone to war a great many times.

Battles and conflicts have long broken out on the border between these two neighbors, mainly over the exact position and layout of the border and ownership of the land and territories along it.

As a result, the border was permanently guarded for a long time by soldiers and garrisons on either side, who would keep a watchful eye on whoever—or whatever!—tried to cross it. And in the fall of 1925, it was one of these border crossings that led to Greece and Bulgaria going to a brief but bloody ten-day war.

Although the precise events that led up to the start of the war are sketchy, according to most versions of this story, a stray dog that just so happened to wander across the border from Greece into Bulgaria was to blame. Other versions claim that the dog was actually owned by one of the Greek soldiers positioned along the border, who then ran across the border to retrieve it.

With tensions high along the border, the dog—and perhaps its owner—crossing from one country to the other, if only for a few minutes, was enough to cause a brief firefight to break out. In the crossfire, at least two Greek soldiers were reportedly killed.

In the days afterward, tensions between the two nations continued to sour, and the situation continued to spiral. The Bulgarian government later apologized, claiming that the entire incident had been nothing more than a misunderstanding. The Greek government, however, wanted the soldier responsible for the shooting to be punished and demanded a cash settlement for the dead men's families. To hammer home their demands, they ordered troops to cross the border and occupy the border town of Petrich, where a raid on the local headquarters of a Bulgarian committee was ordered. In the fighting that ensued, more than 50 local people lost their lives.

After ten days, however, the League of Nations—the international peace-keeping organization that eventually became the UN—stepped in. Tensions between the two sides were quelled, and the War of the Stray Dog was brought to an end.

## THE BATTLE OF DEN HELDER, WHEN HORSES FOUGHT SHIPS

Long before we had cars, trucks, jeeps, and tanks, horses were the most important means of transporting soldiers and equipment to the front line in times of war. At a bizarre battle in 1795, however, soldiers on horseback managed to do a little bit more than just that...

At that time, many of the superpowers of western Europe—including France, Austria, Prussia, the Netherlands, and

Great Britain—were involved in a series of bitter battles and conflicts known as the War of the First Coalition. The war had partly been sparked by the outbreak of the French Revolution in 1791, with many of France's neighboring countries keen to take advantage of the turmoil to claim French territory as their own, while France's ambitious new Revolutionary government was just as keen to make gains of its own in return.

In 1794, French troops pushed across the northern border of France into the neighboring Netherlands, where they eventually succeeded in taking control of the Dutch capital, Amsterdam, the following January. Seeing little chance to fight back, the Dutch government simply announced that the Netherlands would become France's ally—effectively surrendering the country to French control.

An official order was sent out to all Dutch soldiers and sailors stating that the two countries were no longer at war and that no member of the Dutch army or navy should attack any French soldier or vessel from now on. But not everyone in the Netherlands was quite so willing to follow the new rules.

Rumors began to circulate that some Dutch naval vessels, anchored off the Netherlands' North Sea coast, were refusing to give in to the French. Instead, they were planning to set sail across the North Sea to England, where they could ally instead with the British and, together, launch a joint British and Dutch attack on France's north coast.

The French, understandably, could not risk letting these unruly ships leave harbor and had to quash this rebellion before it started. Luckily for them, however, the winter of January 1795 was an especially harsh one.

The French sent a small army, including several mounted cavalrymen, to the Dutch coast and there found many of the rebel ships stuck in the thick ice of the frozen sea. Once the rebel ships had been identified, all the cavalrymen had to do was ride their horses out onto the ice, where they could access the ships as easily as if they were on land!

Covering their horses' hooves with fabric so as to muffle the sound of their approach, the cavalrymen stepped out onto the ice, rode out to the ships, and boarded them. The mounted attack understandably took the Dutch by surprise—this was, after all, the first and only time in history that men on horseback had managed to take control of a fleet of ships!

The Dutch commanders on board ultimately agreed to enter into negotiations with the French, and in doing so swore that they would remain in harbor, even after the ice had melted—ending the rebellion before it had begun.

## THE WAR OF JENKINS' EAR

If the earlier story about the stray dog hadn't already proved it to be true, the story behind the War of Jenkins'

Ear will show that sometimes wars can break out over the most unusual of things.

In 1738, an English seafarer named Captain Robert Jenkins appeared before the British parliament and presented its members with his own amputated ear, pickled in a jar. The ear, Captain Jenkins explained, had been cut off while he was in the West Indies by a band of Spanish *guarda costas*, or coastguards—buccaneering sailors, used by the Spanish to enforce their strict trade laws across the Americas. The guards had apparently boarded Jenkins' ship the *Rebecca*, by force, before ransacking and pillaging it, cutting off his ear (presumably as a warning), and then setting the ship adrift in the Caribbean Sea.

To the British at the time, this bizarre crime—and the equally bizarre body part at the center of it—was the final straw. For too long, the Spanish had been blustering and bullying their way around Britain's Caribbean ports and colonies, imposing ever tougher laws and tariffs on English goods, and it was high time the government acted to put them in their place. Before long, members of the British parliament were campaigning for the prime minister, Robert Walpole, to act. Despite him not being keen to do so at first, the following year Britain went to war with Spain.

For the next nine years, British and Spanish ships and troops clashed in a string of battles fought across the West Indies, mainland America, the North Atlantic, and the Mediterranean. At first, the British secured some early victories by capturing several important Spanish ports and cities. But over time, progress in the so-called War of Jenkins' Ear proved slow, and the entire conflict eventually fizzled out with neither side having achieved much at all!

## THE ISLANDS THAT REMAINED AT WAR FOR 300 YEARS

Often, formal peace treaties are what mark the end of wars and bring fighting to a close. This is an understandably important process and is often overseen by politicians and military leaders from both sides to make sure no mistakes are made. During the English Civil War of the 1600s, however, one rather important mistake was made that would not be fixed for another 300 years!

The English Civil War was fought between the Royalists (supporters of the king, Charles I) and the Parliamentarians (who wanted to do away with Charles' monarchy altogether and replace it with an all-powerful elected parliament instead). Although the complicated circumstances that led to the war had been rumbling on for decades, the Civil War itself officially began in 1642 and lasted for the next nine years.

During that time, the Parliamentarians found some unlikely support for their cause in the Dutch. England and the Netherlands had long been allies, and when the Civil War broke out, the Dutch decided to support the Parliamentarian side (as they appeared to be the most likely to succeed).

This was understandably seen as a betrayal by King Charles and his supporters, who, as well as fighting the Parliamentarians, also began attacking Dutch ships in the English Channel. Fighting a war on two different fronts, both on land and at sea, however, quickly proved too much for the Royalists. By 1651, they were in trouble.

By now, King Charles was dead—beheaded in Whitehall Palace in London in 1649—and the Royalists had been pushed back to the far southwest corner of England, to their final stronghold in the county of Cornwall. From there, however, there was nowhere else to go except to sea, and so many of the final Royalists abandoned mainland England altogether and sailed out to the tiny Isles of Scilly. These are a group of around 50 islands in the North Atlantic, some 30 miles or so off the English coast. At this point, however, the Dutch once more stepped into the fray.

With the Royalists now cornered, the Dutch saw their chance to get revenge for their losses in the English Channel and so declared war on the Isles of Scilly. Twelve Dutch warships sailed from the Netherlands out to the islands and blockaded their ports. They demanded that the Royalists replace the ships they had sunk and pay for the cargo they had destroyed. This situation endured for the next three months, until finally, in June 1651, the islands surrendered to the Parliamentarians. The Royalists had been defeated, and with the Civil War now over, the Dutch fleet was free to sail home.

Amid all the celebrations of the Parliamentarians' victory, however, the Dutch forgot one small thing. They never signed an official treaty ending their war with the Isles of Scilly! As a result, even after the Civil War was over, the Netherlands technically remained at war with the islands—despite not a single bullet or cannonball being fired and not a single life being lost.

As the decades went by, the war soon drifted into history, and the fact that the islands were still at war with the Netherlands quickly became little more than a humorous bit of local folklore. In 1986, however, a local historian named Roy Duncan decided to investigate and wrote to the Dutch Embassy in London asking if there was any truth to the legend. To Duncan's surprise, the ambassador wrote back to say that no official peace treaty could indeed be found, and so the islands had technically still been at war with the Netherlands for the past 335 years!

Thankfully, the ambassador, Jonkheer Huydecoper, was happy to rectify the mistake. In April 1986, he flew out to the Isles of Scilly bearing a lavish scroll that officially brought an end to one of the longest wars in history!

## DID YOU KNOW?

○ The famous Trojan Horse of Greek mythology was only around 10 ft wide. If it were any bigger, it wouldn't have fit through the gates of Troy!

- Spiral staircases in castles usually turn clockwise. It has been suggested that this is because most people are right-handed, making a clockwise staircase easier to defend in battle!
- Edward I of England built an enormous war catapult, large enough to destroy an entire castle. He called it the "Warwolf"!
- King Edward also tested his catapult on Stirling Castle in Scotland—even though the castle had surrendered!
- The deadliest battle in history was the Siege of Leningrad during World War II. More than five million people died as a result of the siege.
- In 1325, two rival cities in Italy went to war with one another after one stole a bucket from the other's well!
- The Battle of Hastings in 1066 didn't actually happen in Hastings but around five miles away—in a town now known as "Battle."
- France declared war on Mexico in 1838, after a French pastry shop was looted by Mexican officials in Tacubaya!
- The first war tank was invented in 1915 and named "Little Willie."
- Despite being in the middle of the biggest war in history, some countries in Europe remained "neutral" during World War I and so did not fight. Spain, Sweden, and Switzerland all kept out of the war.

# CHAPTER 9:
# SCIENTISTS & ENGINEERS

# CHOLERA & THE WATER PUMP

Cholera is a serious medical infection caused by consuming a kind of bacteria that live in contaminated water.

Someone who happens to drink cholera-infested water—often the result of sewage somehow getting into the local water supply—can become very sick very quickly. Without treatment, the infection it causes can be fatal.

In some countries that do not have good sewage systems and high standards of sanitation, cholera can be a terrible problem. It is estimated that as many as four million people become infected with cholera around the world every single year. In more developed countries, however, infections of cholera are extremely rare, but that was not always the case.

In the summer of 1854, dozens of people in the Soho area of central London fell sick from cholera, all at the same time. Over a matter of just a few weeks, the outbreak gradually grew so bad that as many as 600 people are believed to have died as a result. To stop the deaths, the source of the outbreak had to be found quickly.

At that time, scientists and doctors had not yet discovered germs and bacteria, so they were still not entirely sure what caused cholera outbreaks. The most widely believed theory was that the disease was caused, not by drinking contaminated water, but by breathing in contaminated air, or *miasma*. Armed just with this theory, a local physician,

Dr. John Snow, set out to get to the bottom of the case and, with luck, stop the outbreak in its tracks.

Like a medical detective, Dr. Snow started plotting all the known cases of cholera in London on a map of the city. He found that the vast majority of these cases were centered around a handful of streets in Soho. Snow began interviewing the people who lived there to see what, if anything, they had in common. Eventually, one thing kept cropping up in their conversations more than anything else: they had all used a local water pump on the corner of Broad Street and Cambridge Street.

Snow presumed that the pump must somehow be the source of the outbreak and had its handle removed so that no one could use it anymore. Within a matter of days, the number of reported cases of cholera began to drop. Within a matter of weeks, the outbreak was over.

Later, when the pump was investigated more thoroughly, it was found that the well beneath had been dug only a few feet from an ancient cesspit, which had begun to leak sewage and contaminated liquid into the water of the well.

Snow's detective work and the result of his investigation not only saved hundreds of lives but proved that the miasma theory of cholera was incorrect, and that it must instead be a disease of the water supply. He had not only solved the case but had ultimately changed our understanding of infections and disease forever.

# BENJAMIN FRANKLIN'S TURKEY EXPERIMENT

One of America's most well-known statesmen, Benjamin Franklin, was famously one of its greatest scientists and inventors, too. As well as inventing everything from a kind of rocking chair to bifocal spectacle lenses, Franklin was known for his experiments involving electricity. In particular, he was known for the famous experiment in which he supposedly flew a kite, with a metal key attached to it, in a thunderstorm.

In 1750, however, Franklin had another run-in with the power of electricity that also almost ended his life. And this time, it was not a thunderstorm that was to blame for his mishap, but a Christmas turkey!

Franklin's experiments with electricity had led him to believe that electrocution was both the most humane way of killing an animal before butchering it and the best way to preserve the taste of the meat. "Birds killed in this manner," Franklin supposedly once told a friend in their discussion of electrical shocks, were "uncommonly tender" to eat.

To prove his point, Franklin arranged a demonstration at his home in which he would electrocute a live turkey using a charge of static electricity stored in specially designed battery-like vessels known as Leyden jars. Having invited several friends around to watch the display (and to no doubt enjoy a turkey dinner afterward!), Franklin began setting up the experiment and readying the turkey. In the process, however, he happened to touch one of the electrical wires connected to the Leyden jar, and so instead of electrocuting the turkey, he fired the full charge into his hand!

"The flash was very great," Franklin later recounted, "and the crack as loud as a pistol." He had experienced "a universal blow, through my whole body from head to foot," after which there was "a violent, quick shaking of my body." Luckily, Franklin survived the mishap, and after a moment or two, he came to on his kitchen floor—no doubt much to the relief of his dinner guests!

## THE SCIENTIST WHO DISCOVERED THE SPEED OF LIGHT

Albert Einstein was one of the greatest scientists in history. His work in the first few decades of the 20th century improved not only our understanding of space and time but also science and physics as a whole.

But did you know that something that underpins a great deal of Einstein's work—namely, the speed of light—was discovered almost 250 years earlier?

Back then, in the late 1600s, many of the world's greatest scientists believed that there was no speed of light and that instead light speed was infinite. Put another way, as the fastest thing in the universe, there simply was no limit to how fast light could move.

In 1676, however, a Danish astronomer named Ole Rømer noticed something interesting in a series of observations of the moons of Jupiter he had been making over many years.

Jupiter, the largest planet in our solar system, has more than 90 moons in its orbit. The four largest of these—Io, Europa, Ganymede, and Callisto—are known as the Galilean moons, as they were discovered by the legendary Italian astronomer Galileo in the early 17th century.

Rømer had been observing the innermost and second-smallest of these four moons, Io, for several years. As it orbited Jupiter, and as both Jupiter and the Earth carried on their orbits of the sun, the positions of these three bodies in the solar system would sometimes cause Io to become eclipsed by Jupiter—just like the sun becoming eclipsed by the moon here on Earth! But in looking back over his list of eclipses, Rømer noticed that the precise timing of each eclipse wasn't the same.

At times when the Earth's orbit brought it closest to Jupiter, eclipses typically occurred around 11 minutes earlier than they would otherwise be expected. When the Earth was furthest away from Jupiter in its orbit, meanwhile, the eclipse happened around 11 minutes later.

Rømer knew that these differences could have nothing to do with Io itself, which remained locked in place around Jupiter. Instead, he realized something far more impressive: the delay in the eclipses when the Earth was further away from

Jupiter was due to the light coming from Jupiter having further to travel than when the two planets were closer to one another.

If the speed of light were infinite, as most scientists believed at the time of Rømer's work, then there would be no difference in his data at all. His observations proved that light must have a maximum speed, and so it takes longer to travel further, just like everything else in the universe! Incredibly, Rømer could also use his observations to calculate exactly what that speed must be.

Rømer knew, of course, that the Earth orbits the sun in an enormous circle, with the sun at its center. The 11-minute differences between the closest and furthest points in Earth's orbit, he then calculated, must mean that light would take 22 minutes to travel all the way across that circle from one side to the other—that is, the circle's diameter.

Unfortunately, Rømer was working at a time when clocks, telescopes, and other scientific instruments were not quite as accurate as they are today. Not only that, but our understanding of the true size of the bodies in our solar system—and the distances between them—is much better now than it was in the 1600s! As a result, although all his theories were correct, the calculations he and other scientists of the time carried out were not quite accurate. They estimated the speed of light to be 131,000 miles per second, when we know now that it is closer to 186,000 miles.

Nevertheless, Rømer's painstaking work in observing Io and its eclipses—and his cleverness in figuring out that the speed of light was the cause of the differences he was discovering—gave scientists a new understanding of how light moves and just how fast it does so!

## HOW WERE THE PYRAMIDS BUILT?

These days, human beings are capable of some extraordinary feats of engineering. From bridges to skyscrapers, we have been able to construct truly incredible structures (often in some truly incredible environments!).

But many thousands of years ago, humans didn't have diggers, bulldozers, cranes, and everything else you might see on a building site. So how on earth did the Ancient Egyptians manage to move the enormous limestone blocks they needed to build the pyramids? After all, each of the stones used to build the pyramids weighs around $2\frac{1}{2}$ tons. Moving just one of these blocks in an age before machinery would be difficult enough, but the Great Pyramid of Giza alone comprises more than two million of them!

In an attempt to solve this puzzle, historians have put forward lots of different theories over the years. One idea is that the Egyptians attached temporary semicircular pads to the flat sides of the stones, transforming them into enormous cylinders that could then be rolled into place relatively easily. Another theory claims that blocks were held up on long bendable poles, carried by dozens of men, so that the weight of the stone was spread out—rather like the roadway of a suspension bridge!

The most likely theory, however, is that the blocks were simply hauled into place using ropes lashed around the stones that were then pulled by dozens of workmen. This theory has a problem, however: hauling an object as heavy as a pyramid stone across sand would no doubt cause the loose sand to pile up in front of it, preventing it from moving forward (and perhaps even causing it to sink into the desert!). In 2014, however, researchers at the University of Amsterdam solved this problem.

Discovered on a wall of the tomb of an Ancient Egyptian ruler named Djehutihotep—dating from almost 4,000 years ago!—was an image of 172 men hauling a giant stone statue using ropes attached to a wooden sledge. At the front of the sledge stood another man, who was shown pouring water in front of it out of a jug.

For many years, it was presumed that this figure was performing some kind of ritual—perhaps using the water to cleanse the ground over which the giant statue would pass. The researchers, however, thought that perhaps the water had a more practical use. They began testing the process of dragging heavy weights over wet, rather than dry, sand.

To their surprise, the stones moved far more easily. In much the same way that dry sand cannot be used to make a sandcastle, the addition of a little water causes the grains of sand to hold together. The sand then forms a flatter, smoother surface over which the stones could presumably be pulled with relatively little effort!

## THE PONT DU GARD, THE 2000-YEAR-OLD AQUEDUCT

It wasn't just the Egyptians who produced extraordinary structures in the ancient world. The famous Pont du Gard aqueduct in France—built by the Romans around 2,000 years ago—shows that they were just as good at astonishing feats of engineering.

In simple terms, an aqueduct is a large, bridge-like structure over the top of which lies not a road, but a flow of water. The Romans perfected these remarkable structures, as they allowed them to supply fresh water to their towns and cities, often over astonishingly long distances, using nothing more than gravity to move the water down from higher ground.

The Pont du Gard aqueduct was part of a vast network of waterways that the Romans constructed in the south of France (then part of the Roman province of Gaul) to supply the city of Nemausus (modern-day Nîmes). The city's location was not an easy one to supply with water. The closest freshwater lay downhill, at a lower altitude than Nemausus, and so could not be channeled into the city. Instead, the Romans had to look further afield, and they eventually decided on a monumental project that would transport water into Nemausus from a series of natural springs more than 12 miles north of the city.

If an aqueduct were to be constructed in a straight line from the springs to the city, however, it would have to be built across the steep and heavily forested foothills of a nearby mountain range, France's Massif Central. Not only that, but the lay of the land was such that the aqueduct would be so steep that its water flow could not easily be controlled. Plus, the flow would be so turbulent that it would risk eroding and damaging the stone from which it was made.

Instead, a more gradual route across more open ground would have to be found. In the end, even though Nemausus lies 12 miles from the springs supplying it, more than 31 miles of aqueducts had to be constructed in a long, zigzagging route across the French countryside!

The Pont du Gard is just one small part of this immense project but is arguably its most remarkable feature. It consists of more than 40 limestone arches, built one atop the other in three levels, across the very top of which—some 160 ft above the ground—flows the spring water. The aqueduct crosses the local river Gardon and straddles the vast, stony valley through which the river flows for a total length of over 1,000 ft.

Even more incredibly, however, the Romans succeeded in constructing the Pont du Gard so precisely that there is a drop of just 0.39 inches every 600 ft. This ensures that the water continues to flow downhill, due to gravity, without ever flowing too quickly or too turbulently.

One of the greatest architectural and engineering feats of the ancient world, much of the Pont du Gard still stands (although it has long gone unused as a water supply). It is now listed as an official UNESCO World Heritage Site.

## DID YOU KNOW?

- ○ Albert Einstein's love of science came from trying to work out how the magnets in a compass worked when he was a child.
- ○ The scientist Michael Faraday invented inflatable balloons in 1824. Although he originally used them for holding hydrogen gas in his science experiments, they began to be sold as toys and decorations the following year.
- ○ Isaac Newton quit school when he was 12...
- ○ ...while Galileo was so bright he was sent to a university at age 16!
- ○ The scientist Marie Curie was the first woman to win a Nobel Prize and the first person to win a Nobel Prize twice.
- ○ Because he was so good at chemistry, Charles Darwin's childhood nickname was "Gas."
- ○ What Galileo discovered went so much against what was written in the Bible that the church had him arrested.

○ When Albert Einstein died in a hospital in 1955, the only person nearby was a nurse. He muttered his last words in German—but because she could not understand them, no one knows what he said!

○ Thomas Edison's middle name was "Alva."

○ The inventor of X-rays, William Roentgen, tested his discovery by x-raying his wife's hand!

# CHAPTER 10:
# LAST & LATEST –
# FAMOUS LASTS

# THE LAST PERSON TO LEAVE THE *TITANIC*

As the *Titanic* sank in the early hours of April 15, 1912, the ship's 33-year-old chief baker, a British man named Charles Joughin, ordered his fellow kitchen staff to hand out the ship's remaining supply of bread to the people who were getting into the lifeboats.

At around half past midnight, Joughin returned from the ship's kitchens up to the boat deck to assist in getting even more people into lifeboats. As a senior member of the ship's crew, Joughin was assigned to be captain of Lifeboat #10. However, he gave up his place to a steward and remained on board to help more people escape.

Once all the lifeboats had been launched, Joughin returned to his quarters below deck. There, he drank a half-tumbler of strong liquor before heading back up onto the deck, where he threw deckchairs into the water as makeshift flotation devices for anyone unlucky enough not to be in a lifeboat.

With time now running out, Joughin took one more trip below deck to again grab a quick drink. While he was there, the ship snapped in half with a loud crash! Joughin later said it sounded like "part of the ship had buckled." Making his way back up to the deck one final time, Joughin headed to the rear of the ship and held on to the guardrail.

As the ship sank, Joughin clambered onto the opposite side of the rail—looking downwards at the sea—and rode the sinking ship "like an elevator." Having stood at the very back of the ship as it sank, he was therefore the very last person to leave the *Titanic*.

Extraordinarily, Joughin survived the sinking (partly, it has been said, due to the warming effect of the alcohol he consumed just before it went down!). After treading water overnight, he was spotted and hauled into a passing lifeboat at daybreak. Along with his fellow survivors, he was rescued the following morning.

## THE LAST CONVICT IN AUSTRALIA

In the 18th and 19th centuries, criminals in Great Britain were sometimes not put in prison but instead sentenced to be transported—that is, sent thousands of miles to colonies around the world and, in particular, to Australia. In fact, in the 80 years from 1788 to 1868, more than 160,000 people were transported to Australia.

At that time, Australia was under British colonial rule. The criminals who were transported there left their lives behind in England (and Ireland), usually forever. They were seen as a cheap and easy source of labor. As a result, the convicts were quickly put to work in Australia, building the homes, roads, railways, and other things that were needed for the colonies there.

Eventually, transportation came to an end, and criminals were no longer sent to the other side of the world. The very last ship, a transporter named the *Hougoumont*, arrived at the port of Fremantle, near the city of Perth, in Western Australia on January 9, 1868. On board were the very last convicts—all 269 of them—whom England would send there.

After their work in Australia was over, some transported criminals returned home. However, most remained in Australia permanently—either serving the remainder of their sentence in jail or earning their release and making new lives for themselves on the other side of the world. Most did not have the means to make the long journey back home. One of those who stayed was a man named Samuel Speed, who was born in Birmingham, England, in 1841.

Although not much is known about Speed's early life, records show that in 1863, he was found guilty of deliberately setting fire to a hay bale in a farmer's field. After his arrest, it was found that Speed was homeless and had only set the field on fire so that he would be thrown in jail, where he could at least be assured of a meal and a warm bed for the night! In the end, though, Speed's crime was considered serious enough to deserve transportation, and in 1866, he arrived in Australia.

Three years later, in 1869, Speed was released from jail and allowed to live outside of prison in Australia, so long as he found a job and never committed another crime. Both of these rules he followed perfectly, and he lived a long and crime-free life.

In fact, Speed went on to be the last survivor of Australia's transportation system: he died in 1938 at the grand old age of 97!

## THE LAST PONY EXPRESS DELIVERY

The Pony Express was an express mail delivery service that operated in the United States in the mid-19th century.

As its name suggests, the service used a chain of horses and riders to relay mail across the western US—specifically covering the 1,000 miles of frontier lands between St. Joseph, Montana, and Sacramento, California. This immense stretch of territory, divided by the Rocky Mountains, could be covered by riders in just ten days, vastly reducing the amount of time it took for mail to cross from one coast to the other.

The Pony Express was set up in 1860 and ran for the next 18 months. Understandably, it relied heavily on the availability of riders experienced enough with America's wild west to reach their often remote and rather isolated destinations in time, for which they were paid a staggering $125 a month (equivalent to almost $5,000 today!). Those high costs, however, were just one of the reasons why the Pony Express went bankrupt rather rapidly. Another was the invention of the telegraph, which, just one year later, connected the two coasts of America by wires, essentially replacing the need to send mail at all.

The Pony service officially came to an end on October 26, 1861—the same day that the telegraph line linking Sacramento to New York was completed. Mail that had already been posted, however, was allowed to be delivered, with the final Pony Express deliveries arriving at their destinations the following November.

## THE LAST PRISONERS AT THE TOWER OF LONDON

As we've already learned here, the famous Tower of London—now one of England's most popular tourist attractions—was used as a prison for a large part of its history.

Throughout all the years that it was in use, many well-known people were housed in the tower, including the Scottish hero William Wallace in the early 1300s, Anne Boleyn, the second wife of Henry VIII of England, in 1536, and Guy Fawkes, the famous revolutionary who attempted to blow up the Houses of Parliament in the so-called Gunpowder Plot of 1605.

Incredibly, the Tower of London remained in use as a prison right through to the 20th century. During World War II, the Tower was used to house to Germans captured by the Allies—including Rudolf Hess, the deputy leader of Germany's Nazi Party, and the Nazi spy Josef Jakobs (who was the last person in history to be executed at the Tower, in 1941). The Tower's very last prisoners, however, were two very unusual characters indeed.

Twin brothers Ronnie and Reggie Kray were two of the most infamous gangsters of 1950s London. Together, they operated a company of robbers and hitmen known as The Firm, who carried out a string of brutal assaults and murders across the English capital until the brothers' arrest in 1968.

The Krays were not sent to the Tower for being gangsters, though; in fact, they were imprisoned in the Tower of London long before they fully embarked on their crime wave! It was in 1952 that the brothers first had a run-in with the law—they were called up for national service (that is, to be forcefully enlisted in the army) but refused to sign up. Doing so was a crime, and the brothers were briefly held at the Tower before being sent on to a special military prison in the southwest of England.

Their brief spell in the Tower of London, however, was enough to make the Kray twins the Tower's very last inmates. Its use as a prison ended the following year, in 1952, and it has been used merely as a palace and tourist destination ever since.

## THE LAST NEW LANDMASS IN THE WORLD

As odd as it may seem, we're ending this collection of lasts—and indeed, this book of world history—talking about not the old, but the new!

It's a bizarre thought, but thanks to the nonstop shifting of the gigantic rocky plates that make up the surface of the Earth, land is constantly being destroyed and created. Openings in the Earth's surface can cause land to sink downwards into the magma below or, oppositely, can cause magma from within the Earth to rise up and cool, creating new rock and land on the surface.

Incredibly, the creation of new land is continuing even today. In 2023, an undersea volcano off the coast of Japan produced so much molten rock that it eventually piled up above the surface of the water, where it cooled and formed a new island. Although still unnamed, the island is now officially classed as one of the 14,000 or so islands in the entire Japanese group—and is the newest island in the entire world!

# DID YOU KNOW?

○ The last US telegram was sent a lot more recently than you might think. Set up in 1861, the Western Union telegram service officially ended in 2006!

○ The last passenger of the *Titanic* was 97-year-old Millvina Dean, who died in 2009. She was just two months old when the ship sank!

○ The last woolly mammoth died around 4,000 years ago—meaning mammoths were still alive when the Pyramids were being built!

○ The last time the guillotine was used in France was 1977.

○ The last survivor of the American Civil War, Albert Woolson, died in 1956. He was 106 years old.

○ George Washington's last words were "'Tis well!"

○ President John Quincy Adams' last words, meanwhile, were "I am content..."

○ ...and Theodore Roosevelt's last words were spoken to his valet, James. Before going to sleep, he said: "James, will you please put out the light?"

○ The fossils of the last known dinosaur, a triceratops, were discovered in Montana in 2011. They date from 65 million years ago—right before the asteroid that killed the dinosaurs hit the Earth.

○ The last survivor of the Crimean War was a tortoise that was on board one of the ships sent to the conflict in the mid-1850s. It died in 2006!

# CONCLUSION

Phew! And with those last "last" facts, our journey through more than 6,000 years of history is complete. And what a journey it's been!

We've met kings and queens, con artists and swindlers, some of the world's cleverest people, and some of the most deranged, most murderous, and most dangerous, too!

We've found out what life was like in the days of pirates, how toilets came about, and how it all went down in the longest and shortest wars in history.

We've even found out which king you might have been able to beat in a wrestling ring—and how keeping a polar bear as a pet perhaps isn't such a good idea!

Hopefully, the stories and tales we've explored here have given you a taste of the past and an idea of how amazing a subject history can be.

If so, by all means continue exploring; there are lots more fun things to discover about our fascinating past!

Printed in Dunstable, United Kingdom

72347054R00074